Wild Shores

Exploring the Wilderness Areas of Eastern North Carolina

Walter K. Taylor

With photographs by the author

ISBN 1-878086-19-7

Library of Congress Catalog Card Number 93-071244

Printed in the United States of America

On the cover:
Sweetwater Creek, a tributary of the Roanoke River
Photograph by Ken Taylor

Book and page design by Elizabeth House

Down Home Press
P.O. Box 4126
Asheboro, N.C. 27204

This book is dedicated
to the memories of

John Foster
Loren Shepard
and
Hallie Dale.

They were Down East outdoorsmen
who lived in harmony with the land and water.
These Southern gentlemen were
gracious enough to share
what they'd learned over the years.
They'll always be missed,
but never forgotten.

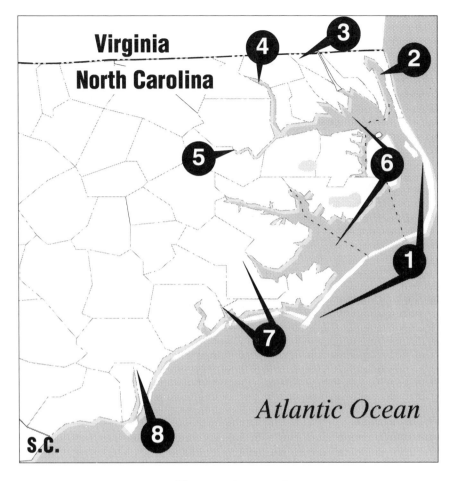

Contents

Introduction

I was born 400 years too late. I should have sailed the unspoiled North Carolina coast with the Roanoke Voyagers. As a boy growing up in Washington, North Carolina, I used to go to the Brown Library just one block away from the Pamlico River to read about those long-ago times.

There were the lusty romantic novels of Inglis Fletcher heralding the adventures of the men who conquered Carolina and the women who loved them. Judge Harry Whedbee wrote of ghost stories, legends and all manner of mysterious and interesting events that occurred along the North Carolina coast. David Stick chronicled the history of the 600-plus shipwrecks in the Atlantic graveyard. Then there were the John White drawings and the accounts of the Roanoke Voyages. John Lawson wrote of his 1,000-mile exploration into the unknown Carolina wilderness. William Byrd wrote so well about the Dismal Swamp that he hated so much.

With my head full of this stuff, after school I'd ride my bicycle down to the riverside dock where I kept an old wooden skiff I'd found after a hurricane and fixed up. In it – powered by pole, paddle, bailing bucket and my imagination – I found adventure in swamps and waterways around my hometown, mounting many expeditions in search of the treasure that Blackbeard the pirate was supposed to have buried in these parts. The swamp woods lured me, too, and I hunted there with an old single-shot twelve-gauge and fished the black waters with a cane pole. I met oldtimers in the woods and on the water and they passed on to me their love and respect for the outdoors.

This love of wild places helped me survive hard times while growing up fatherless during the '60s and it sustains me now. I still go outdoors when in search of peace of mind and inspiration.

I really enjoy the coastal wilds and want to share that good feeling. If more people learn about and enjoy our natural areas, more places will be protected to provide a valuable recreational resource for everyone while keeping our water and air clean. Our wildlife deserves a place to live and we deserve unspoiled natural beauty to enjoy. Besides, it's just plain fun to get outdoors.

Humans have a natural affinity for bodies of water. Millions of dollars are spent on annual migrations to the beach – strips of sand in the shadows of towering condominiums, surrounded by traffic jams, crowds and long lines.

People need a break once in a while from all this civilization. Getting away to the outdoors on weekends and vacations not only revives the spirit of adventure, it builds confidence and renews faith. Time spent outdoors is time spent with the Creator, in my view.

All citizens own waterfront property. National and state wildlife refuges, forests, parks and other public lands are out there for us to enjoy. More than 3,000 miles of shoreline make North Carolina coastal waters an adventurous boater's delight. You can still hunt dinner in the adjoining woods or catch a feast in the water. There are trails to hike, forests to explore, concentrations of wildlife to observe.

Camp by the sea on a barrier island where wild horses roam. Paddle a mysterious blackwater river that twists like a serpent through a cypress forest that was ancient when the first white explorers arrived. Enjoy hiking, swimming and picnicking on a sub-tropical, white-sand beach away from the crowds.

History and mystery linger like the early morning fog on the waters that were traveled by warriors, colonists and buccaneers. Ruins of great battles and traces of lost civilizations tell of lives past.

Many coastal villages are latecomers to the 20th century. Before World War II, many towns could be reached only by boat. Telephones and electricity were rare. Folks who lived here depended on the land and water for survival. They hunted and fished for food. Some of their descendants still do. This is a region on the edge – not only of the land and sea, but of nature and civilization – where the relentless winds and currents collide with the interests of big business and big government.

Too many places have already been ruined by the heavy hands of developers – timeless beauty sacrificed for short-term profits. Some barrier islands are clogged with summertime traffic jams as tourists seek escape from their crowded urban lifestyles. Pulpwood mills, strip mines and corporate farms foul the air and water in the endless quest for the almighty dollar. Leaky septic tanks, sewage systems and highway runoff have polluted many of our once productive wetlands.

Thank God we can still get away from all that, still have places where crowds are absent, the air is good, the water clean and the land unspoiled. Each year a little more land is preserved. People are becoming more aware. They're starting to recycle, clean up waterways and take better care of the land. Things are looking up in North Carolina.

Conservationists through the years have worked hard to make sure we would always have room to experience the freedom of the outdoors. Enjoy these natural treasures, but remember to take good care of these lands and waters so that following generations can still enjoy the wonder of the wild.

Hunting and fishing are the traditional sports of eastern North Carolina, and money from hunters and fishermen has conserved a great deal of the public land mentioned in this book. This area of the state offers one of the widest ranges of hunting available in the country – everything from squirrels and rabbits to black bears – and game is once again plentiful. A lot of eastern Carolina families still put meat on their tables with a gun as their ancestors did.

Fishing is also a treasured heritage here, and there are so many ways to do it. Beginners can learn with cane poles and natural bait in fresh water, then move up to the science of stalking the largemouth bass. You can fish the piers and pilings in the sounds and rivers for flounder or sheepshead, or go after blue marlin in the Gulf Stream. If shellfish are your favorite, you can net crabs, rake clams or hammer oysters from the muck for a feast unequaled for taste and freshness.

All hunters and anglers would do well to consider the words of my friend Fred Bonner, biologist and sportsman. "Success isn't measured in pounds and ounces," he said, "but in the quality of the outdoor experience." Catch or kill only that which you intend to eat.

Those who don't want to hunt or fish but merely observe should consider buying a canoe, the best means of truly seeing the wilds of the North Carolina coast. This land was first settled by canoe thousands of years ago and primitive dugouts made from cypress logs were the most popular form of transportation for many people right up until the Civil War. A few folks in the Green Swamp still use dugouts. There are more miles of water to canoe in eastern North Carolina than there are miles of trails to hike. Larger boats are great for the open waters but size limits where they can go.

I enjoy paddling and watching wildlife or discovering unusual plant life. I can't say that I'm an expert paddler but I still get a kick out of it, and I meet more people doing the same thing every year.

Wildlife watchers need the skill of a hunter. Dress to blend in with the surroundings. Take a bath before going and wash clothes with unscented soap. Avoid perfume or cologne. Move quietly and take advantage of natural cover. Before going, learn all you can about the habits, tracks and signs of the creatures you seek.

Most wildlife is active around dawn and sunset. Good binoculars will add to your enjoyment. Good photography will let you share your adventures with others. Don't harass wildlife. Leave no trace of your presence and perhaps you can return to observe the same creatures again.

Keep a constant watch for snakes during warm weather. This discipline will not only save you from snakebite it also will train your powers of observation and enhance your enjoyment of the wilderness. Defend against insects with protective mesh clothing or a good supply of repellent. Always watch the weather and don't get caught on some remote island during a hurricane or northeaster. Use common sense and observe the proper safety practices. Let someone know where you are going and when you're due back.

Retreat to the wilderness where there are no signs of other humans, only the sound of the wind or the waves or the drone of the forest. It's good medicine. I offer this little guide to help you explore these last stands of wilderness for yourself. Enjoy your journey!

Walter K. Taylor,
On board the Sylvia

For more information about North Carolina, call or write:

N.C. Division of Travel and Tourism. Call (800) VISIT-NC. Ask for Coastal Boating Guide, State Road map and Publication that includes camping information.

N.C. Wildlife Resources Commission
512 N. Salisbury St.
Raleigh, NC 27604-1188

Hunting and Freshwater Fishing License – (919) 733-7846
Motor Boat Registration – (919) 733-7380
East Carolina Game Lands – (919) 638-3000
Report Wildlife Violations – (800) 662-7137

Carolina Adventure (monthly magazine of hunting and fishing in North Carolina)
215 S. McDowell St.
Raleigh, NC 27602
(800) 522-4205 to advertise or subscribe

The Outer Banks

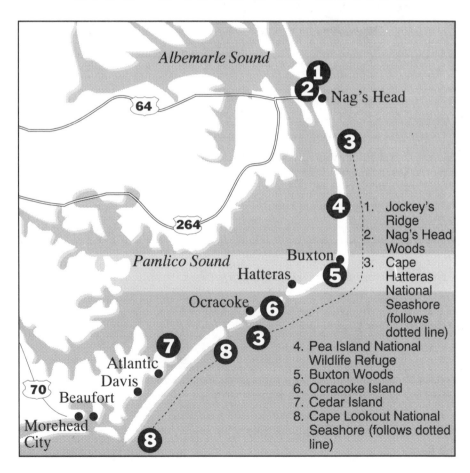

Albemarle Sound

64

Nag's Head

264

Pamlico Sound

Buxton

Hatteras

Ocracoke

Atlantic

Davis

70 Beaufort

Morehead
City

1. Jockey's Ridge
2. Nag's Head Woods
3. Cape Hatteras National Seashore (follows dotted line)
4. Pea Island National Wildlife Refuge
5. Buxton Woods
6. Ocracoke Island
7. Cedar Island
8. Cape Lookout National Seashore (follows dotted line)

Captain Ronnie O'Neal hoists a Spanish mackerel aboard the Miss Kathleen, a 33-foot vessel handcrafted from juniper wood.

It's an autumn dawn on Ocracoke and the salty air is exhilarating. Hurricane Bertha just blew herself out the day before, and Ronnie O'Neal is the first charter captain to leave Silver Lake Harbor since the storm.

He's tall, tanned and lean – likes to wear rock-and-roll t-shirts and looks more like a surfer than a native fishing guide. But his voice is rich with the Old English brogue of the Outer Banks and everybody on the island knows to follow Ronnie to find fish. He comes from a long line of watermen and fishes year-round aboard Miss Kathleen, a Harkers Island boat with that distinctive flared bow for a good ride in heavy seas. His 33-foot craft was handcrafted from juniper wood, powered with twin diesels good for 35 knots.

O'Neal net fishes in the winter but rigs for sportfishing come spring. Anglers come from across the country to try their luck. He's taken blue marlin and once an 800-pound tiger shark.

"After a hard blow like yesterday, it'll take two or three days for the water to get right again," he says. "But don't worry, we'll find some fish."

But first Ocracoke Inlet must be negotiated. The wind is out of the southwest and stirring up a mean-looking wall of breakers between the Atlantic Ocean and Pamlico Sound. O'Neal climbs to the control tower for a commanding view. He leans against the stainless steel railing, braces his bare feet on the cabin roof and studies the pattern of the waves. Spotting an opening, he yells for everybody to hold tight, grips the helm and gooses the throttle. Miss Kathleen races through the thrashing inlet like a diesel surfboard.

That last big wave washes over the cabin windows and then Miss Kathleen rocks gently in the swells like a baby in her mother's lap. The passengers are a little shaken and damp but ready to fish. O'Neal climbs down, sets up the trolling rods and goes to work. At mid-day we return to port with an oversized cooler packed with bluefish, spanish mackerel and flounder. And that's a bad day of fishing on Ocracoke!

No one knows how long Ocracoke Inlet has been a passage between the sea and Pamlico Sound. Inlets come and go with the big storms and hurricanes. This passageway to the ocean has been open at least since 1585 when the first English ship ran aground here, although the southern part of the inlet shoaled over last century and put the village of Portsmouth out of business.

The world's most famous barrier island chain is always changing to suit the sea, not man. This stubborn strip of sand known as the Outer Banks has been holding back the ocean for at least 5,000 years. Flooding from the last Ice Age drowned the lowlands behind this line of coastal dunes, separating them from the mainland and creating a 130-mile long system of long, narrow islands that continue to evolve today.

Like old boxers, the islands roll with the punches of the stormy Atlantic and retreat toward the mainland. Ocean beaches erode on the northern ends of the islands while soundside marshes grow to the south, part of the geological processes of barrier island movement called overwash and littoral drift. Towns and forests have been washed away by the sea in the past. Over-priced beach houses regularly topple into the ocean when the winter northeasters rip into the beaches and dunes. The Banks are long overdue for a major hurricane. Nature is still the final authority here.

"I've long been fascinated with the geology and ecology of the Outer Banks," said John Alexander, naturalist and co-author of *Ribbon of Sand*, a book about the ecology and history of the barrier island chain. He and his biologist partner, James Lazell, have studied the Outer Banks for more than 20 years. "There's a rapid evolution of plants and animals as they adapt to this island movement. It's a fascinating laboratory of evolution. There's no other place like it in the world."

Alexander points out that the sea level has risen three inches in the past decade, and the rise appears to be accelerating. Is this the result of the so-called greenhouse effect, the global warming caused by loss of the protective ozone layer, triggering the melting of the polar ice caps? The research and debate continue as people try to deal with valuable oceanfront property being washed out to sea.

"Jetties, groins, sea walls, they're all just temporary solutions," Alexander said. "In the end, the ocean will have its way. The sea will win."

Ocean beaches are the front lines of this endless conflict between land and sea. Beach grasses such as sea oats find a foothold where the sand piles up high enough. Higher dunes offer shelter from the salty breeze so shrub thickets of yaupon and wax myrtle can take root. The pinnacle of the barrier island succession is the maritime forest with gnarly live oak trees that stubbornly grow despite being stunted and pruned by the salty wind. Even these mature forests can be destroyed by the sea or buried by large moving sand dunes that are driven – one grain at a time – by the ocean winds. All too often people destroy them with bulldozers, concrete and asphalt.

A diverse lot of wildlife lives at the ocean's edge, from the dolphins that frolic just offshore to whitetail deer in the forests and otters in the marsh. Wild island ponies – descendants of shipwreck survivors – live on some islands. The Banks are a major stopover on the Atlantic Flyway for more than 400 species of migrating birds. It's both the northernmost and southernmost limits for many species of plants and animals found in this hemisphere.

Offshore the warm Caribbean waters of the Gulf Stream meet the colder current from Labrador creating ideal conditions for a variety of marine life. That adds up to world-class fishing. World record blue marlin have been caught in the stream. The biggest channel bass and bluefish in the world were caught surf fishing at Hatteras Island. Anglers come from all over to try their luck in these fabled waters.

The islands have always attracted people. Coree and Machapunga Indians paddled across the sounds in dugouts to set up temporary hunting and fishing camps on the Banks. Croatan was a permanent Algonquin village somewhere in the forested section of Hatteras Island now known as Buxton Woods.

The original Outer Bankers are about gone now but they left their mark forever on the islands and waterways they named: Pamlico, Roanoke, Hatteras and Croatan. The natives loved a good oyster roast and left some impressive shell mounds that still stand in isolated spots.

The first Europeans on these shores probably were shipwrecked sailors. One Englishman who was later interviewed by Sir Walter Raleigh reported walking the coast from Florida to Cape Breton before being rescued.

More than 600 vessels are known to rest beneath the nearby waters that mariners called the Graveyard of the Atlantic, victims of storms, shoals, pirates and war.

Italian navigator Giovanni da Verrazano led a French expedition to these shores in 1524 while looking for the Northwest Passage, the mythical short-cut to the Orient, where fortunes could be made in the spice trade. At one point, Verrazano sighted the Pamlico Sound from one of the barrier islands and thought he had found the "Oriental Sea" and the way to the riches of the East. He had trouble getting through the inlets so he sailed further north and never tested his theory.

Phillip Amadas and Arthur Barlowe came in 1584, seeking a base for English privateering operations against the Spanish treasure fleet. Galleons loaded with South American gold rode the Gulf Stream up the coast to the Outer Banks, where they caught the favorable winds and sailed eastward to Spain. Many of these treasure ships were intercepted and captured by British sea dogs such as Sir Richard Grenville and Sir Francis Drake. Quite a few were lost to hurricanes. Galleons full of gold rest now on the ocean floor somewhere off the Outer Banks, just waiting for some treasure hunter.

The English soldiers of fortune met the Indians of Roanoke Island and explored the sounds. They returned to England accompanied by two Indians, Manteo and Wanchese, who made a big hit with Queen Elizabeth with their gifts of Uppowoc, which we now call tobacco. Smooth-talking Sir Walter Raleigh was involved in the Roanoke project and convinced the Queen to authorize the first English settlement in the New World on Roanoke Island.

Raleigh's cousin, Sir Richard Grenville, led seven ships and more than 600 men from Plymouth Harbor in April, 1585. After a rough passage through Ocracoke Inlet, where he almost lost his flagship, he arrived at Roanoke Island. Sir Richard made his own exploration of the region, then sailed back to England, leaving a 100-man garrison under command of Ralph Lane.

Lane's men were more interested in finding treasure than in building a colony. They explored inland and northward to the Chesapeake in search of rumored gold, copper and pearls. Naturalist Thomas Hariot and artist John White went along and chronicled the real treasures of this "goodliest land" – the abundant natural resources. They later published a book about their experiences that is still the definitive report of North Carolina in the late 16th century. White's drawings of the Algonquin people going about their daily lives is our only look at their civilization. Hariot learned the Algonquin language and described the people and their ways in some detail.

The Indians tried to get along with the English and at first traded with them. But the English unintentionally spread smallpox to the natives, who had no natural immunity to the disease. Indians died by the score. The whites robbed Indian fish traps regularly and once burned down an entire village because a silver cup – a gift from the Queen – was stolen from them. Hard feelings grew between the natives and the newcomers. The inevitable war broke out. Governor Ralph Lane called for a truce talk, then treacherously attacked and killed the Indian's chief, Wingina. Lane's men impaled the chief's head on a post and displayed it in front of their fort to frighten and insult the Indians.

Sir Francis Drake's fleet visited the colony on the way home from sacking the Spanish town of St. Augustine and found Lane's men half starved and fearing Indian revenge. Drake supplied the outpost and offered ships and reinforcements, but a hurricane blew in, destroying men and ships alike. Lane's men decided they'd had enough of Roanoke and abandoned their post to return to England with Drake. Grenville's ships arrived two days later to relieve the garrison and found the colony deserted. Eighteen brave souls volunteered to stay behind on Roanoke until help could return.

It was John White, the artist, who returned as governor with 110 people in 1587. His colonists were farmers, artisans and craftsmen with their families, determined to build a new life in the New World. But Roanoke Island was not their first choice. They'd originally planned to settle on Chesapeake Bay with its superior deep-water harbors and only wanted to stop at Roanoke to rescue the men Grenville left behind. But their captain, Simon Ferdinando, was impatient to raid the Spanish treasure fleet and put them out on Roanoke against their wishes. The doomed colonists found the settlement in ruins. Only a few bones remained of Grenville's men, who were never heard from again. It was assumed they'd been killed or chased away by the mainland Indians Ralph Lane had wronged. Manteo's people at Croatan, however, remained friendly to the English.

Food was running low and it was too late in the year to get in a crop so the colonists insisted that Governor White sail back to England for supplies. He became a grandfather before he left when his daughter had a baby girl, Virginia Dare, on August 18, the first child of English parents to be born in the New World.

Governor White returned to England and found the country at war. The Spanish Armada threatened the coast and the queen wouldn't spare a ship to rescue the Roanoke colony. White desperately persisted and finally hitched a ride to Roanoke aboard a privateer in 1588.

He found the colony deserted and his armor rusting in the sand. The word "Croatan" was carved on a tree, a pre-arranged signal that the colony had moved to the village of Manteo's people on the forested part of Hatteras Island. A Maltese cross carved into certain trees was the agreed upon sign indicating danger, but no such cross was found. White wanted to go to Croatan and search for his family and friends but the captain of the privateer had just barely survived a fierce storm and was anxious to leave. Later searchers found no trace of the colonists.

What happened to the lost colony? Did Virginia Dare grow up and have children of her own? Do their descendants live on? These are still mysteries with many theories, but few clues.

Perhaps the Spanish or hostile Indians attacked the island, killing or capturing the settlers. John White always believed they went to live with Manteo's people on Croatan. More than 100 years later John Lawson traveled there and met light skinned, gray-eyed natives who told of white ancestors who could read and write, but it was unclear if they were descended from the colonists or perhaps shipwreck survivors.

English historian David Quinn, the leading expert on the Roanoke Voyages, concluded that the colonists relocated to the Chesapeake Bay and lived among friendly Indians until they were all wiped out by the great warrior chief Powhatan. Isolated groups living in the Green Swamp and along the Lumber River have claimed to be descended from John White's colonists.

We'll never know for sure what happened to the first English colony in the New World, but the spirit of Virginia Dare and the rest of the lost colonists still haunts the state's history. The legend of the Lost Colony lives on every summer with a splendid outdoor drama presented on Roanoke Island near the original site of this colony. This beloved musical play has itself become a cherished Outer Banks tradition.

Englishment of the New World continued, but no one attempted again to settle what is now North Carolina from the sea. The coast was just too risky to navigate and was avoided by all except smugglers and pirates. About the mid-17th century people began moving southward from Virginia, following the rivers to the sounds and settling the high ground. Some moved to the barrier islands, including hermits who sought solitude and lived on nature's provisions.

Most Outer Bankers made a living from farming, fishing and gathering the spoils from shipwrecks. There were an unsavory few who enjoyed shipwrecks so much they started causing them. These land pirates lured vessels to their doom during storms by deceptively placing lights along the shores.

One such group led by Willis Gallup hung a lantern around a scruffy old horse's neck and walked the nag across the dunes to simulate a ship's light bobbing in the waves. It was the custom in those days that when two ships met at sea they would pull alongside to exchange information and supplies. This maritime courtesy was exploited by the land pirates. A captain would steer for the light, thinking a snug anchorage was in sight, then suddenly find himself aground, with the surf pounding the ship to bits while small boats full of cutthroats attacked the crew and passengers. Only one person ever was known to survive these raids, the wife of the governor of South Carolina. She was spared only because she was insane and even pirates thought it was bad luck to kill such a person.

That's one story of how the town of Nags Head got its name, according to Willis' ninth-great-grandson, Kevin Baum, a boatbuilder from nearby Mann's Harbor.

The most notorious pirate of all was the sea-going outlaw Edward Teach, better known as Blackbeard. He was said to stand seven feet tall and he terrorized the Atlantic Coast and the Caribbean. The pirate liked to burn strands of hemp in his dark, luxuriant beard to present a smoky, devilish appearance while leading boarding parties. This fearless buccaneer was quick-tempered, handy with pistol or cutlass and quite a lothario, said to have wives in Edenton, Bath, Ocracoke and who knows where else.

He settled in Bath where he sold his ship, the Queen Anne's Revenge, married a local girl and supposedly gave up his evil ways after receiving a government pardon.

But he couldn't resist temptation and soon built a new ship, the Adventure, and resumed his free-lance privateering operations. Many historians think that Governor Charles Eden knew of the pirate's activities but kept quiet because he was getting a cut of the loot.

A group of Carolina citizens got fed up with this and appealed to the Virginia government for help. Lt. Robert Maynard and a bold force of Royal Marines aboard two shallow-draft sloops were dispatched to deal with Blackbeard.

They found the Adventure at anchor in Ocracoke Inlet, unable to flee to the open sea until the tide came in. The marines attacked and suffered heavy casualties from the Adventure's cannons. In a desperate move, Maynard ordered his surviving troops to hide below deck playing dead. Thus he suckered Blackbeard into boarding his small ship, the Ranger. The pirate and his boarding party were ambushed from behind by the marines. Blackbeard fought like the devil himself after suffering multiple sword and gunshot wounds that would have killed any normal man. Finally, a cutlass stroke beheaded the pirate and his body went over the side. Legend says the headless corpse swam around the ship several times before sinking in the spot still marked on the charts as Teach's Hole. Blackbeard's body and treasure have never been found.

Maynard sailed to Blackbeard's home port in Bath with a trophy — the pirate's head mounted on the bowsprit of his ship — to announce the arrival of law and order to these waters. Blackbeard's skull was reportedly plated with silver and made into a drinking cup.

Taking a drink from this gruesome goblet supposedly gives great power to the imbiber, according to the late Harry Whedbee, a judge and author from Greenville who wrote several successful books about Outer Banks folklore and once drank a toast from the pirate's skull.

Blackbeard's death ended the age of piracy and the British Navy ruled the Outer Banks until the American Revolution. Colonial captains who knew how to get around in these tricky waters made fortunes smuggling European weapons through the British blockade to General George Washington's Continental Army.

During the American Civil War the key battle for the North Carolina coast was fought on Roanoke Island in 1862. The Outer Banks fell early to federal forces under General Ambrose Burnside, who routed the ill-prepared Confederates. Union forces then controlled the sounds of Carolina and went on to conquer the cities of New Bern, Washington and Plymouth. The area remained in Yankee hands until the war's end in 1865 and beyond.

The Union Navy's most powerful ship, the Monitor, survived the epic battle of the ironclads at Hampton Roads, Virginia, but the winter storms off the Outer Banks did what the Confederate Merrimac could not. The "cheese box on a raft" sank in a gale on the last day of 1862 while sailing to Charleston. A Duke University research ship found the Monitor in 220 feet of water about 16 miles offshore in 1973. Just one more watery tomb in the Graveyard of the Atlantic.

The waters of the Outer Banks were feared and cursed by the captains who sailed the coastal trade routes. Passing this area was the most dangerous part of any trip, and the federal government acted to make the sea lanes safer.

A chain of lighthouses was built and manned to warn ships away from the shoals. The most famous of these is the 208-foot Cape Hatteras Lighthouse built in 1873. This commanding structure with the distinctive black and white spiral paint job is a well-known symbol of North Carolina. It, too, now is threatened by the ever-encroaching sea. The National Park Service has decided to move the structure back 2,500 feet at an estimated cost of seven million taxpayer dollars. The job is supposed to be completed by 1995, the economy and weather permitting.

The lighthouses were a great help to navigation, but more was needed. The U.S. Lifesaving Service started with seven lifesaving stations in 1874. Eventually posts were established seven miles apart along the beaches. Crews were made up of local fishermen who knew the water, some of them no doubt descended from the land pirates who plagued the Outer Banks years before. The service operated like a maritime rescue squad. The men trained, maintained equipment and patrolled the beaches on horseback during storms, looking for ships in distress. Lifesaving became a way of life for the Outer Bankers.

The exploits of those salty heroes are legends of bravery and seamanship. If a stricken ship was close to shore, they used a special cannon called a Lyle Gun to fire a grappling hook and rope to the vessel. Once the rope was secured, passengers were evacuated one at a time with a sliding seat called a "breeches buoy." If the ship was further out, the lifesavers had to row out in surfboats to rescue the passengers and crew. All this while battling high winds and heavy seas.

These brave men had a fatalistic attitude about their work. They believed that the rules said they had to go out, but didn't mention coming back. But come back they did, bringing survivors with them. One man, Rasmus Midgett, was patrolling the dunes on horseback and saw a sailboat run aground. He didn't have time to get back to the station for help so he singlehandedly swam out and rescued a dozen survivors, bringing them to the beach one at a time.

Capt. John Midgett, Jr. and the crew of the Chicamacomico station – all but one of them were Midgetts – pulled off the most daring rescue of all, saving 42 British sailors from a burning oil tanker, the Mirlo, after it was torpedoed by a German submarine in 1918. Their lifesaving station is preserved today as a heroes' museum. Reenactment of lifesaving drills are held weekly for summer visitors. The U.S. Lifesaving Service was later incorporated into the U.S. Coast Guard and the lifesaving tradition of the Outer Banks continues today.

There was plenty of rescue work when the Outer Banks became the front lines during both world wars of the 20th century. German U-boats killed at will during the early days of World War II and inspired a deadly new nickname for the Outer Banks, Torpedo Junction. Older residents tell of seeing ships burning offshore while bodies and wreckage washed up on the beach. But the American navy got its licks in and finally took control of the coast. Two of the marauding Nazi submarines are now underwater attractions for scuba divers.

The Outer Banks hosted an unprecedented military buildup during World War II that introduced the barrier islands to the 20th century. Paved roads, bridges, ferries, electricity and telephones came with the war. Tourists and developers followed and have been flocking to the

Surf fishing at Cape Hatteras. In the background you can see the Cape Hatteras Lighthouse.

The Lifesaving Station at Chicamacomico. The crew of the Chicamacomico station rescued 42 British sailors from a burning oil tanker, the Mirlo, after it was torpedoed by a German submarine in 1918. Their lifesaving station is preserved today as a heroes' museum.

Banks ever since, building on every available piece of beachfront property, land considered worthless only a few years earlier. Once isolated Outer Banks communities now boast of traffic jams and urban sprawl to match any beach resort in the country.

But thanks to conservationists there are still places where the solitude and wildness known to the first visitors to the Outer Banks can still be experienced. The more accessible recreational areas get crowded at times, yet there are still islands without bridges and with trails away from the highways. Travelers willing to take a boat ride or a hike can explore a salty wilderness centuries away from modern life.

Today's explorers have to go beyond the highways to find the real Outer Banks but the effort is worth it. The stars are brighter, the clouds whiter and that salt air is still intoxicating here on the edge of the land.

Jockey's Ridge State Park

A major landmark on the Outer Banks is a colossal moving sand pile called Jockey's Ridge near Kitty Hawk. The largest dune on the East Coast, it varies from 110 to 140 feet in height, depending on how the wind shapes it. This unique dune once was used as a natural amphitheater where spectators watched local jockeys race wild ponies in the sand.

Visitors still climb the dune to enjoy the grand view of the northern Outer Banks or to fly kites and model airplanes. The more daring soar on the winds themselves, attached to hang gliders, an appropriate activity here within sight of the spot where the Wright Brothers first achieved motorized flight.

Giovanni Verrazano, an Italian navigator employed by France, was the first European to visit this area he called Arcadia. Algonquin Indians were living here, but it isn't known whether they were permanent or seasonal residents. The French explorers reportedly kidnapped an Indian youth during their brief stay and carried the unfortunate child back to France.

During the early 1800s planters from the mainland came across Albemarle Sound to build resort homes and escape the malaria-ridden swamps. Some settled in the sheltered area of Nags Head Woods and today many of their homeplaces are being reclaimed by the forest.

A grand hotel for two hundred guests was built, complete with a half-mile-long pier to the deep water of the sound and a railroad to the beach. It was destroyed by retreating Confederate troops during the Civil War.

Jockey's Ridge has long been a popular recreational area and lover's getaway. Local people once believed that if a courting couple walked to the top of the dune together they would soon be happily wed.

One woman who climbed the dune in the 1960s saw a bulldozer tearing into the base of the dune, confronted the operator and made him stop. Carolista Baum's bold act inspired local people to get together and stop development from encroaching on the dune. Through their efforts, it was preserved as a state park in 1975.

The public owns 393 acres around the dune open for daytime recreation. No camping is allowed in the park but plenty of private campgrounds are in the immediate area. It's an arduous hike in blowing sand to the top of Jockey's Ridge, but the view is worth it. Tracks in the sand tell of the deer, raccoons and foxes that travel here by night.

From the top, the visitor can get a feel for just how fragile the Outer Banks really are, a narrow ribbon of land between the sea and the sounds. Look west and the base of the dune begins to turn green with shrub thickets and maritime forest before leveling off into marshes at the edge of the sound. The view is spectacular at sunset. To the east is a jumble of structures crowding close to the beach. To the north, the view is of Nags Head Woods, another large dune, Run Hill, and beyond that, the Wright Brothers Memorial.

When I was growing up, my family would park beside Highway 158 and walk up the spectacular dune. Today's park provides a paved parking lot, a natural history center and museum at the ranger's office, where you can pick up maps and brochures. Eight picnic shelters and modern restrooms are convenient to the parking lot.

Follow the path south to climb the dune. Even that is easier now. Local volunteers have built stairs, boardwalks and benches in some places. But be warned: it's still an arduous climb and caution should be exercised on a hot summer day.

Kids love to play in this giant sand box, even older ones. Local high school boys have invented a new sport here – sand boarding. They take the wheels off skateboards and ride them down the sandy slopes.

Seagulls soar around the dunes, often joined by their human counterparts, the hang-gliders. Hang glider rentals and instructions are available at private businesses nearby.

The author's wife, Gwen, and son Eric, study nature at Nags Head Woods.

Nag's Head Woods

Jockey's Ridge and Run Hill provide a break from the wind and salt spray that allows a mature maritime forest to thrive at their bases. Nags Head Woods spreads over 1,400 acres between the two big dunes. Rainwater runoff from the dunes recharges the groundwater and creates ideal conditions for plants and animals that are found nowhere else on the Outer Banks. The woods are still the only source of fresh water for the town of Nags Head.

Tests indicate the woods are more than 1,000 years old. There's a live oak tree known to be 500 years old. The first settlers found a safe haven here from the frequent storms that swept the islands.

A community once grew in the forest. It had two churches and a school, but the last resident moved out in 1948 and nature is being allowed to reclaim the forest. Old family cemeteries deep in the woods hint of a simple way of life dependent on the sea. Folks were superstitious back then.

An old widow who once lived in these woods was thought to be a witch. She had a pier behind her cabin. It was customary for a fishing boat returning home to stop at her dock and leave a few fish. Sometimes, though, a crew would sail right on by and fail to share their catch. The woman would become enraged, set fire to an old mop and run around chanting a curse, before planting the flaming mop in the ground. Within hours the northeast wind would blow a gale and nobody could get out to fish.

Eventually, the local fishermen would figure that someone had angered the old woman and they would go to her house with a load of fish and other gifts. Her anger appeased, she'd remove the mop, the storm would stop and the Outer Bankers could put to sea. They usually had an excellent catch, which they were quick to share with a poor old widow who had no way to catch fish for herself.

These woods still feel a little spooky. The maritime deciduous forest and swamp forest systems found here exist in only five locations in the world, and they're all classified by the Nature Conservancy as endangered. The forest was listed by the U.S. Congress as a National Natural Landmark in 1974. The North Carolina chapter of The Nature Conservancy got started in 1977 and with the help of concerned local people the woods were preserved in 1978.

"It's the most biologically diverse maritime forest in the country," said Jeff Smith, the director of the nature preserve. About 1,100 of the 1,400 acres of woods are now protected from development and logging. The Nature Conservancy owns 400 acres outright and jointly owns another 700 acres with the town of Nags Head.

The preserve is managed by The Nature Conservancy not as a park, but for research, education and limited recreation. The fresh water aquifer beneath the woods provides water to the town of Nags Head. Hunting, fishing and camping are forbidden here. Visitors are allowed at limited times. Call to make arrangements. Conservancy members can visit any time but everyone must register at the office.

Two trails invite hikers to explore the forest. The Center Trail near the office is an easy 1/4-mile stroll that offers a look at some of the habitats in the preserve. The Sweetgum Swamp Trail is the best day hike on the Outer Banks. Its two and a half miles stretch over relict beach dunes and around the swampy bogs and ponds. One section on a high ridge bears trees covered with the thickest mat of Spanish moss I've seen anywhere. Pick up a trail guide at the office to learn of the flora and fauna. Take your time here. There's something new to see around every bend.

Numerous fresh water ponds and swamps are pretty to look at and they host the most diverse population of reptiles and amphibians on the Outer Banks. More than 20 species of snakes are found, including cottonmouths. A wide variety of toads and frogs join in the woodland chorus. Rare salamanders and turtles reside in the ponds.

More than 50 types of birds nest here and hundreds more pass through during annual migrations. Deer, squirrels, raccoons and opossums are common, and the sharp-eyed hiker might see a gray fox or river otter.

Cape Hatteras National Seashore and Pea Island National Wildlife Refuge

Hatteras! The word was a curse to early mariners who came to grief here. But today Hatteras is a blessing for people who love to fish, hunt, watch waterfowl, surf, sail or relax on the beach.

The Cape Hatteras National Seashore was authorized by Congress in 1937, but not until 1953, when money finally became available, was it officially established. This narrow island chain, stretching 72 miles from Bodie Island southward to Ocracoke, offers 30,300 acres of beaches, dunes, grasslands, thickets and the largest maritime forest in North Carolina. The park is broken into several tracts separated by the Pea Island National Wildlife Refuge and six island towns: Rodanthe, Waves, Salvo, Avon, Buxton and Hatteras. This oceanside playground is managed by the National Park Service and is accessible by car except during severe storms or exceptionally high tides that flood roads or close bridges. More than two million visitors enjoy this park each year and the number is growing.

The Park Service operates five campgrounds and numerous roadside beach access sites. But hard times and tight budgets have caused rangers to have to do more with less.

"We'll try to provide as many services as possible in the most cost efficient manner," said Robert Woody, public information officer for the park. "We'll have to concentrate on the busiest part of the year, during the summer."

Park campgrounds are the first to feel the pinch. There are 675 campsites at five different campgrounds. The Bodie Island, Hatteras and Ocracoke campgrounds usually are open from mid-April until the end of October, while the Salvo and Frisco units are open only in the summer. Plenty of privately operated campgrounds are found up and down the Banks, many of them open year-round. For those who don't want to rough it, hotels, condos and cottages are available close by. Reservations likely will be needed for the crowded summer season.

Head south from Nags Head and take a look at the recreational opportunities along the way. Stop at the visitors center at Whalebone for maps and other useful information.

First stop inside the park is at the Coquina Beach Recreation Area, although there's not much left at this writing. A storm at Halloween, 1992, destroyed half of the parking lot and all of the picnic shelters. Park officials are planning to rebuild when money is available. The beach is much closer to the road now. A ramp provides access for off-road vehicles.

The Laura Barnes, one of the last of the sailing schooners, wrecked near here in 1921, and the remains of the wooden hulk were moved to this beach to protect it from the restless sea. Many other shipwrecks may be seen along the park's beaches at low tide, a smokestack here, another piece of rusting wreckage there, tombstones in the Graveyard of the Atlantic. Good fishing can be found around most of these wrecks.

Across the road from this beach is the Bodie (pronounced body) Island Lighthouse. Built in 1872, it is marked with broad horizontal bands of black and white. Each of the five Outer Banks lighthouses has a different paint pattern. That made it easier for ship captains to identify them and know their locations in the days before radar and satellites assisted navigation systems.

The keeper's quarters is maintained as a visitors center. A self-guided boardwalk trail and observation tower beside the adjacent marsh offer excellent waterfowl viewing opportunities. Woods and thickets around the lighthouse road are full of deer and rabbits.

At the end of Bodie Island on the ocean side is the first of the National Park Service campgrounds, and it's typical of the lot. Tents and RV's are set up at marked sites between the dunes. Drinking water and a bathhouse are provided. Campers need lots of mosquito netting for bug free ventilation. Tenters should bring extra-long "sand pegs" to keep tents from blowing away in the usually brisk winds. Some sort of dining fly or canopy is needed for shade since there are no trees.

Hatteras camping allows access to relatively unspoiled beaches with all modern conveniences close by. Campground hours and rates are subject to change and reservations will be needed during the busy summer season, so call ahead.

It's an easy walk to the beach for fishing or swimming. Swimmers need to be aware of the rip currents that can wash them out to sea if they're not careful. Watch children closely. It's always a good idea to monitor the weather forecasts on the radio and avoid swimming when the water is rough or a storm is passing close by. Read and observe the posted swimming information or consult a ranger.

When the wind gets up and the big waves start crashing on the beach the surfers get excited. These waves have hosted world championship surfing events and earned Hatteras a place of honor in the surfing world. Shops abound in the area for surfers and board sailors, who find the windy Pamlico Sound a paradise.

All types of watersports equipment can be rented up and down the beach: kayaks, canoes, sailboats, Hobie Cats, jet skis. Waterway traffic can get crazy during the summer. Operate with consideration for others and the environment.

The big tourist crowds thin out when the weather cools. That's when the ducks and geese arrive. Duck hunters live for the days when the northeast winds of winter start "spittin' snow" across the Outer Banks. Loaded down with decoys, calls, shotguns and Thermos jugs of steaming coffee, they wade through the marsh before dawn, setting up decoy rigs and scanning the skies for flocks of ducks.

Once they're spotted it's up to the caller to bring them into shotgun range. Dogs fetch the downed birds, and day's end brings fresh duck dinners and the camaraderie of the hunt. It's an Outer Banks tradition that endures.

Twenty blinds are provided on Bodie Island for waterfowl hunters to use in season. Duck hunters can set up portable blinds in the soundside marshes on park service land all the way to Ocracoke. Jump shooters can prowl the marshes for targets of opportunity, but they must keep at least 300 yards from any blind. Shotguns must be plugged to allow only three shells in the magazine. Only steel shot may be used. The marshes are well patrolled, and violators of the rules will be charged.

There's usually an October season for the abundant teal and December and January seasons for widgeons, pintails, mallards, black ducks and snow geese. Hunting for the once abundant Canada geese was closed in eastern Carolina in 1992. Duck hunting seasons and regulations change frequently and waterfowlers should always call ahead for up-to-date information.

Oregon Inlet is a passage to the sea that opened during a hurricane in 1846 and was named for the first vessel to sail through it. In 1963, the Herbert C. Bonner Bridge extended Highway 12 across the inlet to Hatteras. Before that, ferries were the only way across. Island residents got a reminder of those good old days during the winter of 1990 when a storm blew a dredge ship into the bridge and knocked out a 200-foot chunk. Highway transportation and electricity to island residents stopped cold. Once again, Hatteras Island was cut off from the rest of the world until the State Department of Transportation put in an emergency ferry service that ran until the bridge was repaired.

Commercial and sports fishermen pass through the inlet en route to the rich fishing grounds, but it's a troublesome passage. Hardly a year goes by without somebody running aground on the sandbars. Some days no one can get through. Commercial fishermen want the Army Corps of Engineers to build a multi-million dollar pair of jetties to stabilize the inlet, if that's possible. Park service officials and environmentalists oppose the project, fearing increased beach erosion south of the jetties. Once again, the ocean does its own thing while humans fret.

At the foot of the bridge is the Oregon Inlet Fishing Center, a world-class base for saltwater fishing. Several record blue marlin of more than 1,000 pounds have been taken in the Gulf Stream by the fishing fleet here. The all-tackle world record blue marlin was caught here in 1974, weighing in at 1,142 pounds. White marlin and sailfish are frequently landed.

A popular and tasty gamefish often caught here is the yellowfin tuna, which sometimes reaches 300 pounds. Wahoo, king mackerel, big bluefish, amberjack, albacore, other varieties of tuna and sharks round out the offshore fishing. Crews on the 35 charter boats here are usually locals with great experience on these waters.

The best deal going for a family on a budget or for novice fishers is a half-day inshore trip aboard one of the headboats. Bait, tackle and the skipper's expertise are provided for about $20 per person. Passengers on these boats often catch coolersful of blues, croakers, spots, sea trout, Spanish mackerel and other fish, depending on the weather and luck. It's probably the best way for people new to coastal fishing to learn its fundamentals and have a chance at a good catch. The fishing center operates as a concession for the park service and has a complete marina, restaurant, tackle shop and fish-cleaning service. Charter fleets also operate from Roanoke Island, Hatteras and Ocracoke.

Those who want to fish the inlet without paying can do so from the catwalks of the Bonner Bridge. Boat ramps also are available.

The first 13 miles of Hatteras Island lie within the Pea Island National Wildlife Refuge, which offers shelter to migrating waterfowl,

Snow geese return every winter to the Pea Island National Wildlife Refuge.

birds and aquatic mammals and reptiles. This place is reserved for birders. No guns or hunting allowed.

It's a great place for a family adventure, like a giant bird feeder. Four miles of trails around the intensely managed impoundments offer camera and binocular hunters a good look at the flocks of migrating waterfowl that descend on the marsh every winter. Observation towers make it easy to get an overall view of the ponds and marshes. You can easily observe thousands of birds during the fall and winter migrations.

Snow geese return every winter accompanied by Canada geese, swans and assorted ducks, all attracted by well-managed food plots in the refuge. Predators such as osprey, eagles and peregrine falcons pass through. Egrets and herons find something to eat in the wetlands year-round. Otters and turtles share the marsh with the birds and the mullets.

Stop at the information booth, grab a map and follow the trail markers from the parking lot. Call ahead and the refuge staff can arrange guided trips for groups. The trail is paved and level across the marsh and can accommodate wheelchairs for part of the way.

There's still a lot of beach left between here and Hatteras Inlet.

Most people simply drive the highway and take advantage of the access areas. Hikers can walk the beach and the many side trails. More four-wheel-drive vehicles and all-terrain vehicles ride the beaches every year.

Most of these off-roaders come to fish in the surf, hoping to get blitzed by a school of tackle-busting bluefish or to fight a 90-pound channel bass to the beach. There are 22 ramps to the beach that off-roaders are required to use. Most drivers deflate their tires to 10 or 15 pounds pressure for maximum traction on the sand. Speed limit on the beach is 35 mph but drops to 15 mph when pedestrians are near.

Driving on the dunes is prohibited at all times to protect nesting areas of the endangered piping plover. Whole sections of beach may be closed at times to protect turtle nests or because of excessive erosion.

Jeep-type vehicles need proper licenses and insurance to operate on the beach. Smaller all-terrain cycles have to be operated by licensed drivers. Park rangers patrol the beaches and don't mind writing tickets.

In early spring and late fall, fury hits these beaches. Vast schools of voracious bluefish move in, herding schools of bait fish such as menhaden and mullet toward the beach, then slashing into them in a savage feeding frenzy. Gulls and pelicans clean up the scraps.

Anglers watch the birds to find the fish. When they spot them, the cry goes out on the Hatteras grapevine. The blues are running! Jeeps and trucks move in and the bluefish blitz is on. Anglers use long rods, 10 to 12 feet long, and reels loaded with 20-pound test line. Shiny metal lures such as Hopkins, Stingsilver or Clarkspoons are the preferred artificial bait but have to be attached to wire leaders because the toothy blues will bite right through the line. When the blitz is in full swing fishers can pick up all the natural bait they want at their feet, as the terrified small fish flop onto the beach trying to escape the bluefish. Feeding blues don't care what they bite, as some fishermen have learned the hard way after extracting their mangled fingers from a chopper blue's mouth.

It's the most exciting surf fishing experience there is – landing bluefish that weigh between 10 and 15 pounds one right after the other. There's usually a spring run around Easter, then the big fish return in the fall, fat and sassy after feeding all summer. Doesn't take any special skill to catch blues, just be there when they're running.

Not so for the big channel bass, the supreme challenge for surf anglers. It takes patience and time to catch what the local folks call drum. The younger fish known as puppy drum weigh only a few pounds, but big drum may run to 50 pounds.

Drum like rough, muddy water and fresh, oily cut bait such as mullet. The big ones usually bite at night but any kind of light will spook them. Skates, stingrays and sharks are also apt to hit cut bait and any of these can provide an exciting fight.

Surf anglers land smaller fish – spot, croaker, whiting (called Virginia mullet locally), gray trout and flounder – from spring through fall and usually enjoy a good run of pompano in the late summer. Pier anglers catch all these but also have a shot at king mackerel, tarpon, cobia and the occasional surprise. Eight fishing piers are to be found along the Cape Hatteras National Seashore.

Wading the shallow waters of the sound with a fly rod or spinning outfit is starting to catch on here. Some nice puppy drum and speckled trout are caught by waders. Small boaters in the sound work the channels and deep holes. A good skipper with a shallow-running boat usually can find some big blues around the sand bars near Oregon Inlet. Catching big blues on light tackle is a real thrill. Fishing is the number-one sport on Hatteras Island, and there are many ways to enjoy it.

Buxton Woods

In the shadow of the Cape Hatteras Lighthouse is the largest maritime forest remaining in North Carolina, the 3,000-acre Buxton Woods. This is where Chief Manteo's people are believed to have lived and perhaps where the Lost Colonists of Roanoke Island ended up. About 900 acres of the forest are owned by the National Park Service, the rest by the state and various private owners. Local citizens mounted a grass roots effort during the 1970s to save the woods from being bulldozed into a golf course and housing development. Through their efforts, about 2,600 acres of natural land were saved.

Like Nags Head Woods, this forest recharges the ground water. It supplies the only fresh water from Avon to Hatteras Inlet. Tight regulations control development here to conserve this precious water source. Only one house can be built per acre. Wetlands can't be filled. The relict dunes can't be bulldozed, and the cutting of trees is strictly regulated. Nine wells in the 500 acre state-owned part of the forest are strictly monitored. There's concern that drawing too much water from these wells will dry out Jeannete's Sedge, a 400-acre pond, the largest fresh water wetland found on an East Coast barrier island.

Visitors to Buxton Woods find welcome shade and a chance to glimpse a vanishing habitat only a short distance from the beach. "It's beautiful year-round," said Marcia Lyons, the National Park Service naturalist here for nearly 20 years. "It's thirty miles from the mainland and all life here is controlled by the maritime elements."

Live oak, yaupon, holly, red cedar and flowering dogwoods are shielded from the continuous salt spray by overgrown relict dunes. Dwarf palmettos at the northern limit of their range add a slightly tropical look to the forest.

There's more diversity of mammals here than in any maritime forest in the state, everything from rice rats to deer. Peregrine falcons and bald eagles roost here during their migrations. Reptiles and amphibians inhabit Jeannette's Sedge. Wildlife from the surrounding area finds shelter in the woods during the frequent storms and floods that ravage the island. Hunting and fishing are not allowed.

There's a 3/4-mile self-guided trail for visitors to experience the woods. A shady picnic ground is at the trail head. Interpretive hikes are guided by rangers during the summer and special arrangements can be made for groups that call ahead. Heavy rains bring out the mosquitoes, even in daytime, so bringing repellent is advised. Stay on the trail and look out for cottonmouths. Camping is available in season at the Cape Point Campground operated by the Park Service or year-round at private campgrounds in the area.

No trip to Hatteras Island is complete without a visit to this special forest. Here you still get a feel for how the island used to be.

Ocracoke

Hatteras Island ends at Hatteras Inlet and motorists can take a free 40-minute ride on the state-operated ferry to the island of Ocracoke, the jewel of the Cape Hatteras National Seashore. No bridge connects this island to the mainland. It's almost a three-hour ferry ride across the boisterous Pamlico Sound to either Swan Quarter, northwest on the mainland, or Cedar Island to the southwest. Ocracoke natives like it that way. They don't want their island getting overcrowded like Hatteras.

"I don't know about all these Yankees coming down to the Outer Banks and buying up everything," said Capt. Junius Austin, an Ocracoke charter-boat operator. "There's a lot of money being made, but we're losing a special way of life."

Ocracokers are some of the friendliest folks in the world but they have a stubborn tradition of independence. The islanders want to secede from Hyde County – with its county seat of Swan Quarter located on the mainland – and become part of Dare County. They resent the long ferry ride to the county seat and feel that their mainland county government is out of touch with the island people of Ocracoke.

There's no disputing the beauty of Ocracoke's 12-mile beach. No building is allowed along the beach. All development is restricted to the ferry landing on the north end of the island, which is rapidly eroding away, and Ocracoke Village on the more stable southern end.

The Park Service offers a campground and beach access on the outskirts of the village. An interpretive center is at Silver Lake Harbor in the village. The wild ponies that once ranged over the island are now kept in a pen near the Hatteras ferry landing to protect them from the traffic on Highway 12.

Ocracoke has seen a lot of changes over the years as more vacation homes and hotels have been built, but the quiet seaside village still retains much of the laid-back charm of an earlier age.

Many of the houses and shops here are partially constructed from salvaged shipwreck timbers. The oldest lighthouse still in use in North Carolina is at the southern end of the village. On sandy Howard Street, live oaks stand watch over old family cemeteries. The Coast Guard maintains a small burial ground for four British sailors whose bodies washed ashore after their ship was torpedoed by a German submarine during World War II. This bit of ground has been formally deeded to Great Britain and is officially considered English soil. Tourists who don't like to walk can see the sights from the Ocracoke Trolley.

Talented islanders sometimes put on a locally produced and written musical at the island school about their most notorious former resident, Blackbeard, and his last days on Ocracoke. It's a lot of fun and profits from this excellent show go to the island medical center.

Kayaks can be rented for exploring the marshes and tidal creeks, where many deserted little beaches and shady islands can be found. Otters and long legged wading birds share these waters. Pelicans nest on small islands in Ocracoke Inlet. Cold weather brings ducks and geese. Hot weather means mosquitoes, so bring plenty of repellent.

Charter boats run from Silver Lake Harbor, which is dominated by the ferry landing and the Coast Guard station. Guides can be hired for the excellent fishing and waterfowl hunting. Sailboats can be booked for sightseeing or romantic sunset cruises. More adventurous souls can take a boat trip across the inlet to the deserted village of Portsmouth.

Comfortable hotels and romantic little pubs surround the scenic harbor. Yachts and commercial fishing boats dock here. This is no place to get in a hurry, just a place for relaxing and letting the sea breezes blow away cares. That's the charm and magic of Ocracoke.

Horseback riding is a perfect way to see the best of Cedar Island. In the background is the Ocracoke Ferry.

Cedar Island

It's almost a three-hour ride on the state ferry from Ocracoke to this spit of land that marks the southern end of Pamlico Sound. Most drivers keep going down Highway 12 but there's a little-used wilderness to explore right here.

The Cedar Island National Wildlife refuge keeps on growing. Established in 1964, it now contains 10,000 acres of salt marsh and 2,450 acres of soundside woodlands. And land acquisition continues.

Highway 12 runs for six miles through the waving needlerush and cordgrass marshes of the refuge. Roadside observers will see thousands of gulls and terns nesting here in the summer. Jellyfish and crabs can be seen in the canals. Egrets, bitterns, herons, rails and other birds hunt among the clumps of saltgrass that they share with reptiles and amphibians. Huge flocks of redheads return in the fall, accompanied by other diving ducks such as buffleheads and scaup. A few hundred black ducks nest here in the spring and a special study is being done to determine the effects of low-flying military aircraft from the Naval Air Station at Cherry Point on these scarce waterfowl.

Longleaf, loblolly and pond pine dominate the woods with an occasional pretty stand of live oak. Some deer roam here and residents report seeing an occasional bear crossing the road.

Headquarters for the refuge is at a former Navy radar station near Lola. A scenic picnic area overlooks Core Sound beside an abandoned radar tower that would make a splendid wildlife observation tower if someone would fix it up. There's a boat ramp at the end of the road and that's it for visitor facilities.

But leave it to free enterprise. Next door to the ferry landing is the perfect way to see the best of Cedar Island – an island-hopping horseback ride.

"It's like living inside a painting," said Wayland Cato, artist and polo player turned boss of White Sand Trail Rides.

He urged his horse into Snake Channel as our group of riders followed. Our sturdy quarter horses swam to the next island and climbed the dunes with ease. Flights of pelicans cruised by. Herds of wild ponies grazed in the distance. Occasionally a spooked rabbit darted away at the sound of hooves.

Our mounts preferred to wade in the sound where the breezes kept pesky flies away. We spotted a herd of wild cattle. Cato swears the cows have developed web feet from living in the marsh. The shy cattle faded into the shrub thickets like overgrown deer, but their tracks weren't webbed. Cato not only spins tales about web-footed cows, he tells of mullet graveyards and other products of his artist's imagination – just to keep everybody entertained and happy.

Cato made his name and fortune by mastering the nearly forgotten art of glass engraving with a stone wheel. He's sold his works to Jimmy Carter, Henry Kissinger, Anwar Sadat, Bob Hope and many other collectors. Ducks Unlimited commissioned him to create a set of glass vases with portraits of waterfowl carved into the surface.

He comes from a Charlotte family of avid horse enthusiasts, and is an accomplished polo player. Originally he brought his string of polo ponies to Atlantic Beach with the intention of forming a team, but the city fathers decided they didn't want horses on the beach.

Dejected and disgusted, Cato went riding with a friend on this private string of islands on Pamlico Sound – and he was hooked. In short order he acquired land, built a barn, hired guides and offered his horses for hire.

Riders can chose from gentle mounts suitable for beginners or the more spirited polo ponies. His guides love their work and are dedicated to giving their clients a memorable experience. Cato has exclusive lease to 2,000 acres that border the wildlife refuge and is planning to offer overnight camping trips to Hog Island sometime in late 1993. He even dreams that one day horses will replace four-wheel-drive vehicles as the main transportation along the beaches of the Outer Banks and he's trying to convert the Park Service to his way of thinking.

During the full moons of May and October Cato opens his domain to people who want to bring their own horses for a full weekend of activities, including live entertainment and, of course, lots of riding. A motel, restaurant and store just across the road offer accommodations and supplies. A shady private campground is an easy walk from the barn and offers beach hiking and a boat ramp. This is the place for those who've dreamed of taking a romantic horseback ride by moonlight on a white sand beach. Just keep out of the mullet graveyard.

Cape Lookout National Seashore

South of Ocracoke is what I consider to be the real Outer Banks today – the Cape Lookout National Seashore. No bridges connect North Core Banks (also known as Portsmouth Island), South Core Banks and Shackleford Banks to each other or to the mainland. As it has ever been, a boat ride across the sound is the only way to get to this national park.

These islands, encompassing 27,870 acres, were acquired by the federal government 1975. Not everyone hereabouts was happy about it. Local fishers and hunters had makeshift cabins on the Banks. The Park Service considered them squatters and destroyed the cabins. Subsequently, some Park Service structures were mysteriously burned and arson was suspected.

This national seashore is not as accessible as the one to the north at Hatteras, but officials estimate that 500,000 visitors make the salty pilgrimage here each year. Most come by private boat.

"Visitors have to plan their visit here," said Ranger Eve Kwiatkowski. "But if you want to walk on a beach without seeing another person for miles, this is the place to do it. Fall is the best time to come. It's prime fishing season and the weather is more comfortable."

Headquarters for this park is at Harkers Island, where a visitors center is being built on 90 acres with a picnic area and self-guided nature trails. Ferries debark from Harkers Island for Cape Lookout on South Core Banks and Shackleford Banks. But visitors to North Core Banks must seek access elsewhere.

Portsmouth Village is a ghost town at the northern end of Portsmouth Island, across the inlet from Ocracoke, where private boat owners offer transportation. For about $15, Capt. Junius Austin at O'Neal's dockside store will carry you across the sound to adventure. Established in 1753, Portsmouth once was a prosperous seaport. Ships docked here to transfer cargo to shallow-draft vessels that could sail across the tricky Pamlico Sound to the mainland ports of Washington, Bath and New Bern.

Before the Civil War the south side of the inlet started shoaling over and the ships couldn't get through any more so they took their business elsewhere. When the war started, all the island residents fled as Union troops invaded, except, according to folklore, one woman who was said to be too fat to get through the door of her house.

The town never really recovered and residents gradually died or moved away. In the early 1970s, two elderly women and one man were the only remaining inhabitants. When the old man died, the women reluctantly left the island to live with relatives on the mainland. Margaret Babb, the last surviving full-time resident of Portsmouth, lives now in Beaufort and returns to her former island home from time to time.

Many of Portsmouth's houses are still standing along with the life-saving station and the church, which hosts an occasional wedding. Caretakers employed by the park service live here during the summer months to watch over this historic village. Portsmouth is such a contrast from the overbuilt beach towns to the north that it is a must see for the visitor who wants to experience the isolation and primitive beauty of the real Outer Banks.

There's no store on the island, nor is there mosquito control. Visitors must bring everything with them. Primitive camping is allowed outside the village. Twenty-three miles of wild beaches offer plenty of solitude. The night skies are remarkable for the stars that seem so near and bright, undimmed by any artificial light.

Near the southern end of Portsmouth Island at Long Point is a rustic fishing camp operated as a Park Service concession. Here Don Morris carries on a tradition begun by his father, who founded this camp back in the 1940s. His father hauled the lumber across Core Sound in a 20-foot open sailboat and built the first primitive cabin, still in use today.

"When I was 16 years old Daddy left me out on the island to look after the place," Morris said. "I had an old rusted-out T-model Ford to get around on. They used to catch a lot of fish in those days. I've seen them catch pickup loads of drum."

Back then vehicles were hauled to the island on a barge and abandoned when they quit running, gradually turning the island into a sandy junkyard.

The Cape Lookout Mobile Sportsfishing Club joined with the U.S.

Don Morris operates a private ferry back and forth across Core Sound, from Don's Marina near Atlantic on the Carteret County mainland to a fishing camp on Portsmouth Island.

The oldest cabin at Portsmouth Island Fishing Camp was built in the 1940s with lumber hauled from the mainland in a 20-foot sailboat.

Marines and hauled away more than 500 of the rusting hulks with fork lifts, helicopters and barges after the Park Service acquired the land, and the beach looks much better now.

Morris hauls four-wheel-drive vehicles and passengers back and forth across Core Sound to his camp on his 48-foot Harkers Island-built wooden ferry, the Green Grass. He leaves from Don's Marina near Atlantic on the Carteret County mainland.

The ride over usually is uneventful, but it can be rough when the northeast wind is blowing hard and waves begin breaking over the deck. There is no maintained channel to the island. Morris has marked a route through the shallows with long pieces of plastic pipe stuck into the bottom. The Green Grass creates its own channel from the prop wash by following the same route through the shoals all the time.

The cabins at the camp have few modern conveniences. Propane gas supplies light, heat, refrigeration and hot water. No phones or electricity, but the caretaker has radio contact with the mainland. Groceries, bait, ice, beer and other essentials are ordered from the caretaker and delivered on the daily ferry runs. No cable TV or pizza delivery at this beach.

Big ringneck pheasants live in the marshy grasslands behind the cabins. A pack of robber raccoons has gotten adept at opening coolers and doors in their eternal search for food. Mosquitoes and bloodthirsty greenhead flies feast on those who forget their insect repellent. No venomous snakes are known to be here or on any of the islands of the Cape Lookout National Seashore.

Dedicated surf fishers happily make the pilgrimage to Portsmouth Island. "We like it out here. It's like being on Gilligan's Island," said Mike Warwick of Sanford, who brings his friends here to surf fish every year. "We like to rough it, and these drum sure are fun to catch."

Don Morris says anybody who's willing to work at it can catch a lot of fish here. Anglers need to fish around the clock when they first arrive to figure out when and where the fish are biting. Once patterns are established, they can rest at the cabin and return to the same spot at the same time every day to catch all they want. Some anglers just stay on the beach with four-wheel-drive campers. They sometimes fill up coolers while others are in the cabins. The cabins were built close to some productive drum holes, however, and it's possible to catch a lot of fish within walking distance of the front door.

Red drum is the most popular catch here. The island record is 70 pounds, 12 ounces. Drums in the 30- to 50-pound range are caught almost daily during the height of the fall season. Blues, trout and floun-

31

der are caught in the waves. Anybody who tires of surf fishing usually can find success gigging for flounder in the sound.

Rules for beach driving here are basically the same as at the Cape Hatteras National Seashore. There's one uncharted island on the north end of the beach that's connected to the main island by a narrow sandbar at low tide. One unlucky fellow ventured out there after dark, got caught by the incoming tide and ended up driving into the ocean. All that could be seen of his truck was an antenna until the waves covered that too. Several nice flounder were caught around this temporary artificial reef until it was finally towed out.

Across Drum Inlet from Portsmouth Island is South Core Banks. The inlet is barely usable, an Army Corps of Engineers boondoggle that requires constant expensive dredging. Disgruntled locals call it the "political ditch."

Alger Willis operates a similar surf-fishing camp on South Core Banks. Access is by private ferry from the fishing village of Davis on the mainland in Carteret County.

For additional information on costs of ferry rides and location of camps, see the listings at the end of this chapter.

At the southern end of South Core Banks, Cape Lookout bends into the Atlantic like a giant fish hook. This creates a bay called the Cape Lookout Bight, an excellent anchorage and fishing hole. The bight once was used by Spanish privateers who ambushed ships sailing from the mainland port of Beaufort.

Cape Lookout is not much different now than it was when John Lawson wrote in 1709 of Coree Indian whale hunters who camped here. The Indians would spot a whale just offshore and paddle after it in dugout canoes. When they caught up with it, a plucky warrior would climb onto the whale's back and plug the blow hole so the whale couldn't submerge. The animal could then be killed and towed to shore, where the meat fed a whole village for months.

Later, a whaling and fishing center called Diamond City grew here until the great storm of 1899 washed it away. The site is now underwater in Barden Inlet. Not even the dead were spared during the big blow of '99. The sea unearthed caskets from the graveyards and scattered them about the island. Most survivors moved across the sound – the fortunate ones floated their houses over on improvised barges – to the more protected Harkers Island and Bogue Banks, where many of their descendants remain.

Visitors who take the ferry to Cape Lookout during summer months can ride a trailer pulled by a farm tractor to the beaches from the dock for $3 to $6 – depending on how far you go. Tent camping is allowed and there is no charge. The best place for it is a grove of windswept pines between the dock and the beach planted by former Cape Lookout residents Les and Sally Moore. Hikers can explore shipwrecks and old cannon emplacements along the shore. See the end of the chapter for information about ferry schedules.

Shackleford Banks nestles behind Cape Lookout and is unique for having an east-west orientation to the sea, offering some shelter from the prevailing winds. It is a designated wilderness area and no vehicles of any kind are allowed on the island. This is my favorite place to camp in the park. This island has more maritime forest here than on the others, providing plenty of shade. If you should camp here, just make sure the ponies aren't using the spot you choose.

On one trip to the island I encountered a Shackleford stallion with a bad attitude. He didn't like my kayak floating so close to his herd in the salt marsh. He stomped, snorted and shook his shaggy mane in warning. I had no desire to fight a wild horse with a paddle so I did the only sensible thing and retreated.

Fresh water marshes and ponds have evolved on the sound side of the island and provide a natural haven for waterfowl. Back Sound is shallow, making it a perfect spot for flounder giggers. Horseshoe crabs, resembling some kind of medieval armor, spawn here in the spring and are fascinating to watch. Caution is advised for boaters here, for the sound's many shoals and shallows make it treacherous.

A hike across Shackleford Banks reveals sun-bleached tree trunks where a once lush forest was overwashed by the sea. The wild horses gallop across the dunes at the approach of people. Beaches are wide, clean and crowded with gulls, skimmers and terns. Loggerhead sea turtles crawl from the sea on summer nights to lay their eggs. The only development on the island is a Park Service dock and hand-pump well.

Ticks and mosquitoes are plentiful but rangers report no venomous snakes on the island. Non-aggressive gopher snakes and black racers are sometimes seen.

The western end of the Shackleford Banks wilderness is considered the southern terminus of the Outer Banks. Less than a mile away across Beaufort Inlet lie the heavily developed and densely populated Bogue Banks. A four-lane highway dissects Bogue Banks connected by a brace of bridges to the Carteret County mainland.

Between Shackleford Banks and the town of Beaufort stretch more than 2,000 acres of salt marsh and sandy islands, part of the Rachel Carson sanctuary, named for the author of *Silent Spring*, the book that inspired the modern environmental movement in the 1960s. Carson did research in this area and wrote a book, *The Edge of the Sea*, based on her work here.

Cape Lookout National Seashore is a time capsule allowing us to experience this wilderness at the edge of the sea much as it was before people ever set foot on these pristine islands, offering refreshment for body and soul.

For more information about the Outer Banks:

N.C. Aquarium/ Roanoke Island
PO Box 967
Manteo, N.C. 27954
(919) 473-3493
Marine life exhibits and scheduled field trips aboard 28-foot pontoon boat.

Jockey's Ridge State Park
PO Box 592
Nags Head, N.C. 27959
(919) 441-7132
Annual Hang Gliding Spectacular, the oldest hang gliding competition in the country, held here every May. Annual Rogallo Kite Festival in June offers competition in children's, homebuilt and stunt kites.

Nags Head Woods Preserve
PO Box 1942
Kill Devil Hills, N.C. 27948
(919) 441-2525
Self guiding nature trails but open limited hours so always call first.

Cape Hatteras National Seashore
Route 1, Box 675
Manteo, N.C. 27954
(919) 473-2111
Contact in advance for campground reservations and waterfowl hunting information. Also administers the Fort Raleigh and Wright Brothers historical sites. Ask for schedule and rates for Lost Colony Outdoor Drama.

Ocracoke Civic Club
Ocracoke Island, N.C. 27960
(919) 928-6711
Fishing, camping, boating and lodging information. Crab Festival on the waterfront in May, featuring crab races, crafts and other entertainment. Ask about locally produced musical about Blackbeard. Proceeds go to the island medical center.

Cape Lookout National Seashore
PO Box 690
Beaufort, N.C. 28516
(919) 728-2121
Rates and schedules for ferries and the two surf-fishing camps that operate as Park Service concessions on North and South Core Banks. In general, ferry rates run $12 round trip for an adult passenger, half that for children. $60 round trip for a standard vehicle under 18 1/2 feet long. Passenger ferries leave from Harkers Island and the Beaufort Waterfront. Vehicle ferries carry four cars and leave from Atlantic and Davis. Usually no scheduled ferry runs in the winter months. Access then by private boat only.

Cabin rates vary according to the size of the cabins and the number of occupants, starting from $20 for a 4-man cabin to $120 for a 12-man cabin.

Morris Marina, Kabin Kamps and Ferry
1000 Morris Marina Rd.
Atlantic, N.C. 28511
(919) 225-4261 for reservations. Serves North Core Banks.

Alger G. Willis Fishing Camps, Inc.
PO Box 234
Davis, N.C. 28524
(919) 729-2791 for reservations. Serves South Core Banks.

White Sand Trail Rides
PO Box 1040
Atlantic Beach, N.C. 28512
(919) 729-0911
Located on Cedar Island beside the Ocracoke ferry dock. Campground, motel, store and cafe convenient to the stables. Call for reservations and further information.

N.C. Aquarium/Pine Knoll Shores
PO Box 580
Atlantic Beach, N.C. 28512
(919) 247-4003
Sea life exhibits and scheduled field trips. Next door to 265 acre
Theodore Roosevelt Natural Area. Hiking trails explore the last remnant of unspoiled maritime forest on the heavily developed island of
Bogue Banks.

Core Sound Decoy Guild & Festival
PO Box 308
Harkers Island, N.C. 28531
(919) 728-7316
Sponsors popular annual decoy festival on Harkers Island in December. Working to establish a wildlife museum to celebrate the waterfowling heritage.

North Carolina Maritime Museum
315 Front St.
Beaufort, N.C. 28516
(919) 728-7317
Features exhibits about the coast and is a showcase for traditional boat
building. Sponsors annual wooden boat show in April. Scheduled field
trips during the year to study the maritime environment.

The Mailboat
PO Box 3
Harkers Island, N.C. 28531
(919) 728-4644
Award winning quarterly magazine about coastal history and folklore.

Fort Macon State Park
PO Box 127
Atlantic Beach, N.C. 28512
Civil War fort with picnic grounds and beach access on Bogue Banks.

Currituck Sound

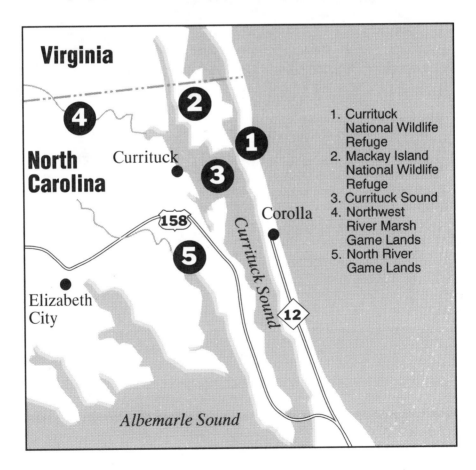

Virginia

North Carolina

Currituck

Elizabeth City

Corolla

Currituck Sound

Albemarle Sound

158

12

1. Currituck National Wildlife Refuge
2. Mackay Island National Wildlife Refuge
3. Currituck Sound
4. Northwest River Marsh Game Lands
5. North River Game Lands

Wild horses and Canada geese are just two of the wildlife species found in the Currituck National Wildlife Refuge, established in 1983 with help from the Nature Conservancy.

Wild geese called at dawn. A flying wedge of 50 or so crossed the rising sun as I paddled across Currituck Sound. About halfway to Swan Island a fog closed in and visibility dropped to less than 50 feet in shoal waters. No problem for a shallow-running canoe. I just followed the duck blinds, one colonized by a pair of surprised barn owls.

With chart, compass and dead reckoning I found the creek that used to be an inlet. A pair of wild horses barely noticed my misty arrival on the last stretch of unspoiled Outer Banks north of Corolla – a fragile slice of land caught between developers and the deep blue sea.

Currituck National Wildlife Refuge was established in 1983 with help from the Nature Conservancy. Formerly owned by two hunting clubs, these lands provide sanctuary for wintering waterfowl. Feral horses and pigs graze in the grasslands and shrub thickets, competing with the native deer. Endangered piping plovers and loggerhead sea turtles are making their last stands in the dunes and on the beach.

The 1,787 acres of refuge land are divided into three tracts of dunes, thickets, marshes and maritime forest. Along with neighboring land owned by the state, the Audubon Society and the Nature Conservancy, a total of 2,807 acres are protected.

There are no marked trails or facilities of any kind. Visitors need permission and a low-impact attitude to legally enter for nature study and photography. Access is by private boat from the cottonmouth-infested sound or by parking a four-wheel-drive vehicle on the beach and hiking through the chigger-rich thickets.

No vehicles are permitted in the refuge. Irresponsible all-terrain-vehicle riders occasionally blast through on their noisy and destructive toys. They're worse than the pigs for tearing up the dunes and vegetation. Mike Panz, the refuge enforcement officer, keeps a close eye for these pig-headed hoodlums and isn't reluctant to arrest them, or any other violators.

These outlaw trail riders are destroying critical habitat for the endangered piping plover. This small, sandy colored bird nests and feeds near beaches. Its feathers are perfect camouflage and blend with the terrain. The birds narrowly escaped extinction earlier this century when they were hunted for their plumage.

Hunting these birds was outlawed in 1918 and the population recovered. But beachfront development following World War II destroyed nesting areas and the piping plover population crashed again. Recent estimates place it at fewer than 1,000 along the entire Atlantic coast from Newfoundland to South Carolina.

Nesting sites are marked and even foot traffic is forbidden in these areas. Still, uncontrolled pets kill and harass the birds. Garbage left by thoughtless litterers also attracts scavenging predators such as raccoons that prey on the nests.

These same predators join ghost crabs to feed on the baby loggerhead sea turtles. Mother turtles crawl on the beaches during summer nights, lay their eggs and return to the sea. When the young turtles hatch, they instinctively head for the ocean. Sometimes they don't get past the tire tracks.

Four-wheel-drive commuters use the beach to reach the private homes north of the refuge. The beach is posted for speed and patrolled, but that is little help to the wildlife that makes the beach its home.

Another wildlife preserve within Currituck Sound is Mackay Island National Wildlife Refuge. It is easier to get to than the Currituck refuge. Drive through Virginia on State Road 605 or take a 45-minute ferry ride to Knotts Island from Currituck. Refuge headquarters – John Kitchen's former hunting lodge – is located off of the Knotts Island Causeway (SR 605). This headquarters also serves the Currituck refuge and is the place to get visitor permits.

More than 9,000 acres of marsh and woods wait to be explored on Knotts Island, a peninsula that straddles the state line. Day visitors come for hiking and wildlife observation. Anglers go for catfish, bass, bream and crabs. Deer hunters with special permits are welcomed during a limited season. Motorists enjoy watching the 25,000 or so greater snow geese that winter in the marsh beside the causeway. Hiking and bicycle trails are open most of the year but closed in winter so the ducks won't be disturbed.

Elizabeth Souheaver manages the Currituck and Mackay Island refuges. A Florida native, she's the only female refuge manager in North Carolina. She worked her way up from a summer job at the Merritt Island Refuge beside the Kennedy Space Center in central Florida. "We have a host of beautiful birds to see," she said. "People come out and hike or bicycle on the trails. They enjoy being outdoors in the natural beauty."

The Mackay refuge was recently expanded with the addition of 1,340 acres of marsh along the northwestern boundary. Future plans call for an improved visitors center and an intensively managed marsh area designed to attract a greater diversity of birds for easier public viewing.

Conserving this refuge is going to require restricting septic tanks and improving the quality of the water in Currituck Sound, according to Souheaver.

Currituck Sound is 35 miles long and ranges in width from four to 15 miles. Brackish, shallow and grassy, the sound is 40 miles from the nearest outlet to the ocean, Oregon Inlet.

The sound's shoreline, nearly pristine not so many years ago, is now dense with vacation homes and condominiums. Marshes are thick with faded pollution markers stuck in the mud by the state. The turbid water used to be clear. Oldtimers had no problem seeing a bass or a crab on the bottom when they prowled the sound in their younger days. Aquatic grass beds that were once thick enough for ducks to walk across are dying. Civilization has not been kind to the sound.

The estuary was far saltier and wilder in 1566 when a Spanish expedition en route to the Chesapeake Bay sought shelter from bad weather on the open sea. Domingo Fernandez skillfully sailed through an inlet – long closed – north of Roanoke Island. Señor Fernandez is thought to be the same Portuguese pilot known as Simon Fernandez on whom Sir Walter Raleigh depended to guide English colonists to Roanoke Island almost 20 years later.

The Spaniards landed on the Currituck peninsula, erected a wooden cross and claimed the land for Spain. They explored the area and left, no doubt disappointed at not finding gold or other valuables. They never even met the Poteskeet Indians who called this place Currituck, land of the wild geese. Indian burial mounds and artifacts were discovered in 1989 that are estimated to be 600 to 900 years old.

Francis Yeardley claimed the land for England in 1654. Planters moved south from Virginia, drawn by cheap land with rich soil. In 1761, John Mackie bought a tract then known as Orphans Island and lived there until he died in 1823. A local legend says that Mackie was buried standing up so he could look out over his fields on what came to be called Mackay Island.

John Lawson, first surveyor general for the North Carolina colony, wrote in 1709 that Currituck Inlet marked the border between the North Carolina and Virginia colonies. With easy access to the sea, Currituck became one of the original ports of Carolina. Ships from around the world came here to trade. In 1728, Colonel William Byrd II drew the dividing line between North Carolina and Virginia westward from the inlet.

A marsh scene at the Currituck National Wildlife Refuge.

That same year Old Currituck inlet closed. Exactly 100 years later, New Currituck Inlet shoaled over and cut off Currituck Sound from the ocean. Fed by fresh water rivers, the sound turned brackish. Aquatic plants such as wild celery grew in abundance in the new environment. Ducks and geese soon discovered this feeding bonanza and came in great flocks.

Ducks became the major industry in Currituck. The flocks returned every winter when farming was off and fishing slow. People then thought of ducks as an abundant natural resource to get them through the winter.

Market gunners baited the marshes with corn and stalked them at night with bright lanterns mounted on their boats. The lights stunned the sleeping ducks and made them sitting targets. A few gunners used small cannons called punt guns that killed hundreds of birds with one blast. Most used repeating shotguns. The birds were cleaned, packed in special ice barrels and shipped north on the Albemarle & Chesapeake Canal to be devoured in fine restaurants and hotel dining rooms. Local folks liked to eat the small black ducks called coots or bluepeters, which still are preferred by many Currituck oldtimers.

"It was a way of life for the old people of this area," said Wayne Waterfield, a third generation decoy carver and duck hunter whose grandfather was one of the original market hunters. "In those days, you either farmed, fished, duck hunted or trapped, or all of the above. There was no business or industry in Currituck County then."

Sport shooters got wind of all those ducks and flocked to Currituck. One party discovered the good hunting by accident.

Gene Wade of Knotts Island is the caretaker and chief guide for the Swan Island Hunting Club, as his father and grandfather were before him. He met me at the dock as I paddled up and told me how the club got started.

A group of New York duck hunters set out in the fall of 1872 aboard their sailboat, the Anonyana, bound for Florida. Like so many sailors before them, they got caught in one of the fierce northeasters that rip the Outer Banks every fall and winter.

New Currituck Inlet had been closed since 1828 but the storm blew it open. The Anonyana made it through and found safe anchorage on the lee side of Swan Island.

When the high water receded, the Anonyana was aground and the inlet was closed. The crew made the best of things and hunted around the boat. They ended up having the best duck hunting trip of their lives. For the next seven years, they returned every season to hunt from their stranded vessel. After the boat caught fire and burned, the hunters bought Swan Island and erected a clubhouse there that is still in use. The tower atop the building used to have a heavy long-range rifle mounted there to discourage poachers. The 80-year-old Lombardy poplar towering in front of three-story building is a familiar landmark to Currituck Sound boaters.

Waterfowl hunting, said to be a "gentleman's sport," became a boon to the Currituck economy. And what a sport it was! Guides would lure the geese and ducks into shotgun range with skillful calls and hand carved decoys. Gunners waited in the blinds for the right moment to fire. Hitting ducks on the wing is still the ultimate wingshooting challenge. Sport hunting was unlike the ambush tactics of market hunting – the birds had an excellent chance to escape their human predators. Well trained dogs retrieved the downed birds from the cold waters. At day's end the hunters would feast on duck dinners, toast their hits and curse their misses.

These wealthy hunters bought thousands of acres of land to use as private game preserves and erected elaborate structures to provide comforts on their trips. They hired local men to guide them on their hunts and to serve as caretakers. Men who were handy with guns and fists enlisted as "marsh guards" to keep poachers out. They were the forerunners of today's wildlife enforcement officers. Scuffles and shootouts were common during the so-called "duck wars" that erupted over shooting rights.

Modern conservation techniques were introduced by the hunting clubs. Crops were planted to feed the waterfowl. Areas were set aside where hunting was banned to give the birds a chance to replenish. According to William Neal Conoley, author of *Waterfowl Heritage*, the definitive book of North Carolina waterfowl hunting, most clubs actually raised more ducks than they shot. It had been feared that market gunning would wipe out the duck populations before the practice was outlawed in 1918, but sport hunters stepped in to save the ducks.

One such man was Joseph Palmer Knapp, a duck hunter from New York who made a fortune publishing Ladies Home Journal and investing in the insurance business. He loved duck hunting and he loved Currituck.

Knapp founded Ducks Unlimited, the largest and oldest waterfowl conservation organization in the world. His concern didn't stop with ducks. With his own money, he built a school for the children of Knotts Island, then sought and hired the best teachers in the country and made the fledgling Currituck County school system a statewide leader in education.

Knapp, who died in 1951 and whose ashes are buried near Moyock, is well remembered in Currituck to this day. In 1961, his private preserve at Live Oak Point and that of his neighbor, U.S. Steel magnate William Corey, became the Mackay Island National Wildlife Refuge. The foundation set up by Knapp is still acquiring new land for the refuge.

While duck hunting occupied attentions in Currituck Sound in winter, bass fishing became the passion for the rest of the year. Largemouth bass – known locally as chubs – were despised and thrown overboard by old-time net fishermen. Then sporting anglers discovered the aggressive gamefish in the sound, and Currituck became a magnet for the sport, even drawing professional sports fishermen. The sound was the site of the 1975 Bass Master's Classic, the most prestigious tournament of all, and record-breaking catches were made, further spreading the sound's reputation as one of the country's best spots for bass fishing.

Retired merchant seaman Vance Aydlett was a bass fishing guide before he went to sea in the '60s. He lives in his camper at the Barne's Family Campground on Knotts Island.

"I got ten dollars a day back then to shove two men through the marsh in an old juniper skiff," he said, recalling his days as a guide. "They had the first artificial lures I ever saw. They'd catch nice stringers of bass with a jitterbug or a Johnson spoon. It was some good fishing the last five or six years I guided. Today, good luck!"

His son, Vance Jr. enjoyed growing up on the sound. "Used to come home every day after school and shoot some birds, catch a mess of crabs or do a little trapping," he said. "It was a way of life."

"There has to be an end to all this development some time," said the elder Vance, "or our kids won't know what it's like to catch a fish or crab, or just see clouds of canvasbacks, geese and redheads like when I was a barefoot schoolboy."

"It all comes down to the two E's," said Bill Prevott of Currituck, a hunting guide, campground operator and world champion goose caller. "The environment and the economy, and the economy usually wins."

Bill is a former member of a conservation committee in Currituck County. A man of conscience, he quit, claiming the committee had turned greedy and sold out to developers. According to Bill, environmental regulations were routinely violated by wealthy builders. If the real estate hustlers did get caught by a government agency, they just paid the fine – the equivalent of a slap on the wrist – wrote it off as a business expense and went on their way, he said. Development began polluting the sound.

Then came the drought of 1985 that reduced the flow of the rivers feeding the sound. Without the fresh water, the estuary got too salty for bass and the aquatic vegetation they depended on. As the grass beds died off, the water became more turbid. Combined with pollution, it looked like the end for Currituck Sound.

But Bill believes things will get better. Rain has been good recently and the salinity is dropping. Grass beds are slowly returning and more bass are spawning. "The oldtimers tell me that there have always been cycles of good and bad fishing," Bill said. "It just takes time." Time and more undisturbed wetlands to filter the tainted water.

The Mackay Island refuge is mostly marsh with some upland pine and hardwood forests along with agricultural fields. The Fish & Wildlife Service built artificial wetlands by flooding timber with dikes and pumps, then planting aquatic vegetation for waterfowl. Ospreys perch in dead trees and fish the well stocked impoundments.

The 6.5-mile-long Live Oak Trail circles three of these impoundments and is open to bicycle and foot traffic. The trail actually is a dirt road, frequently traveled by refuge vehicles and tractors during the week. Mackay Island Trail is a four-mile loop around East Pond. Both trails are open during daylight hours from March 15 through October 15. Visitors may hike or bike to the first gate the rest of the year. The refuge roads are open to automobiles for one Saturday in December. This schedule is designed to protect feeding and resting areas for the migratory birds.

The canals and marshes beside the trail are full of herons and egrets. These birds were almost hunted into extinction by the turn of the 20th century. Their bright feathers were in demand for fashionable hats. People finally decided the feathers looked better on the birds and stopped the silly practice.

The refuge has a thriving osprey population. Wood ducks, known as summer ducks in these parts, are year-round residents. Bald eagles make rare appearances. Altogether 174 species of birds have been sighted and 51 are known to nest here.

Turtles and snakes inhabit the canals beside the trails. Agkistrodon piscivoris, also known as cottonmouth or water moccasin, is the dominant reptile here. Always keep a watch for these aggressive pit vipers and their smaller copperheaded cousins.

Nutria, a South American water rodent accidentally introduced to the area in 1941 as part of a failed fur ranching scheme, muskrats and otters make their homes in the waterways. Raccoons and deer are seen in the woods.

Fall and winter are the most exciting seasons here, for that is when the huge flocks of greater snow geese cover the skies. The Knotts Island Causeway offers the best view of these annual visitors. Motorists often park along the road to watch them. The causeway is popular with bicyclists not only in fall and winter but year-round.

Off the causeway is the Great Marsh Trail, a 1/3-mile

Nutria, a South American water rodent, was introduced to the Currituck Sound area as part of a failed fur ranching scheme. It now thrives in the area.

loop around a horseshoe-shaped pond. There used to be a beer joint on this site where drunken shootouts were common. The pond was dug for the bar's customers to fish in. Today it's a peaceful spot. I watched big, prehistoric-looking gar spawn in the shallows of the pond the last time I went and had a good time panfishing with light tackle. The trail around this pond is the only one in the refuge open year-round.

Crabbing and fishing are allowed in the refuge. Bream fishing in the creeks is good. White perch and catfish are caught in the sound. One fellow caught a 30-pound catfish in Corey's Ditch, a canal that crosses the refuge and the causeway.

Limited deer hunting is an important wildlife management tool to prevent overgrazing in the refuge and keep the deer herd free from disease. The season consists of the last two weeks in October and the first two weeks in November. Shotguns, bows and muzzle-loading rifles are allowed. Only 45 hunters – selected by lottery – are allowed to hunt in strictly designated areas. In 1991, 90 deer were taken, the best an eight-point buck weighing 182 pounds.

Hunters have to check in at 5:00 a.m. Hunting hours are from one-half hour before sunrise to one-half hour after sunset. Deer must be tagged when killed and brought to the check station before leaving the refuge. Hunters need a valid North Carolina hunting license and are subject to all state and federal wildlife laws.

No hunting is allowed on the Currituck refuge, which is a shame. The feral pig population is ruining critical piping plover habitat and tearing up rare plants. Controlled hunting could thin out these descendants of domestic pigs that really belong in pens. Hunting hogs used to be the sporting way to start a Carolina pig pickin' in these parts.

"Best pork I ever had," said Bill Prevott, recalling those hunts. "They live on acorns and root in the marsh for tubers. Good eating, but they have to be skinned like a deer, have to get all that fat off."

Waterfowl hunting is not allowed on refuge property but private hunting clubs and commercial guide services still carry on the Currituck duck hunting tradition on private lands.

The state owns two game lands in Currituck County but only skillful boaters can get to them. Logs, snags and stumps tear at the outboard motor propellers of those boaters who attempt to reach them. A good wind can whip up some big water. A shallow-draft boat with plenty of freeboard is the craft of choice for these waters.

A raccoon climbs a tree in the Northwest River Marsh Game Land.

The Northwest River Marsh Game Land is 1,251 acres of wild swamp forest and marshes surrounded by private land between Moyock and Gibbs Woods. Canoes and small jon boats can put in at the end of State Road 1231, paddle across the river and be there in minutes. Trailered boats have to be launched at the Tulls Creek landing on State Road 1222. From the landing head north across Tull Bay about a mile to the mouth of the Northwest River then travel about four twisty miles upstream. Just look for the familiar North Carolina Wildlife emblems on the trees that mark the game land boundaries. No roads lead here.

But the Atlantic Flyway passes right over this refuge and it's heavy with traffic in the fall and winter. Mallards, black ducks and other puddle ducks hide out on this swampy little river. Ospreys keep watch from atop dead standing timber. Eagles pass through occasionally. Wading shorebirds frequent the shallow marshes.

Otters, minks, muskrats, raccoons and squirrels are common, as are cottontail rabbits and big marsh rabbits called bluetails. An occasional bear might wander in from the nearby Dismal Swamp. Only a few deer inhabit the woods. Hunters will need valid N.C. license and a game lands permit. Wildlife lovers should bring a camera and binoculars for this scenic old-growth wilderness. Go after hunting season and you'll probably have it all to yourself.

North River Game Lands is an 8,730-acre-tract that can be reached from the Intracoastal Waterway at Coinjock. It's surrounded by private land and there are no roads. It's only 20 miles from the ocean here and high winds are common so have enough boat for the job. The river is rough around the edges with plenty of submerged timber and stumps that provide excellent structure for bass but can tear up an outboard motor. Go easy through here.

Puddle ducks, diving ducks, swans and geese can all be found here in the winter, along with plenty of timber doodlers, better known as woodcocks. This is a bear sanctuary and the population is healthy and growing. A lucky visitor in spring or summer might spot a mama bear and her cubs, but keep a safe distance.

More than 1,000 acres of this swamp forest is registered as a North Carolina natural heritage area. Large stands of cypress still exist here that have never known the logger's saw. A cypress canopy 80 to 100 feet high covers much of this area, and some giants tower 120 feet above the swamp.

Marshes bordering the rivers and creeks boast a wide variety of grasses: black needlerush, cordgrass, sawgrass, bullrushes and others. The marshes are home to numerous furbearers and wading shorebirds and more than a few snakes. Ospreys perch in the tall cypress, and bald eagle sightings are on the increase. This may be the best place to experience the natural heritage of Currituck.

More than 1,000 people gather at Currituck High School every September to celebrate that heritage. They look at hand-made decoys and wildlife art and watch carving and calling contests, including the World Championship Swan Calling competition. They come not only to celebrate the waterfowl hunting tradition that got their forefathers through hard times but to write a new chapter in that history. The Currituck Wildlife Guild is working to establish a new wildlife museum at the old Whalehead Hunting Lodge next door to Corolla Lighthouse.

Wilson Snowden, who heads the museum committee of the guild, told how the idea came about. "Went to a wildlife show up on the Eastern Shore and stopped by a wildlife museum on the way home," he said. "I noticed right away that most of the decoys on display were from Currituck. We decided we needed our own museum right here at home to preserve our heritage and artistry."

They're getting closer to that goal all the time. A major setback right now is that leaking fuel tanks have been discovered on the property. The current owners have to fix this problem to comply with environmental regulations before the transfer can be made. The money to

The Corolla Lighthouse

buy and renovate the lodge – which is in rough condition – will come from a lodging tax levied on all resort rental property in the county.

"The real estate developers didn't appreciate that too much," said Wilson. "But once the museum is complete, it could be the biggest tourist draw they've ever had."

The clubhouse was built in 1925 by E.C. Knight of Philadelphia and is considered the grandest of the Currituck hunting clubs. Knight got upset because the other Currituck clubs wouldn't let his wife hunt so he started his own. It's listed on the National Register of Historic Buildings. Twenty-eight acres of land and boat slips on the sound come with the lodge.

The guild already owns an extensive collection of hunting memorabilia and needs only a place to display it. The collection includes boats, blinds, decoys, guns and the last remaining sink box on the East Coast. The sink box was a blind that was sunk to be level with the water. Hunters were completely hidden from the unsuspecting ducks and geese until they were in range. It was such an effective device that it was banned in the 1930s. The guild's most recent acquisition is a collection of 251 antique decoys formerly owned by Dr. Neal Conoley, author of *Waterfowl Heritage*, the definitive reference book of North Carolina decoys. When the museum finally opens, displays will be rotated annually so visitors can view a different exhibit every year.

The land and marsh surrounding the museum also will be put to good use. Nature trails will be built and boat rides will be offered. Plans call for the museum to become a center for environmental education, historical research and outdoor recreation.

Currituck people love their marshy land, and all it takes to understand why is hearing just once that high, lonesome call of the wild goose echoing across the water.

For more information about the Currituck Sound:

Mackay Island and Currituck Banks
National Wildlife Refuges
PO Box 39
Knotts Island, N.C. 27950
(919) 429-3100
Group tours can be arranged in advance. Special permission needed to visit the Currituck Refuge. No camping on refuge but staff can direct you to private campgrounds close-by.

Currituck Wildlife Guild
Box 91
Shawboro, N.C. 27973
Organizes annual Currituck Wildlife Festival every September. Working to establish museum beside the Corolla lighthouse. Can provide hunting, fishing and camping information upon request.

Northwest River Park and Campground
1733 Indian Creek Road, Route 168 South
Chesapeake, Va. 23323
(804) 421-7401
Tent and RV camping. Rent a canoe to explore the swampy river. Northwest River Marsh Game Land is about four miles downstream in North Carolina.

Currituck Sports Inc.
PO Box 106
Highway 158
Coinjock, N.C.
(919) 453-4700
Hunting and fishing supplies convenient to North River Game Land. Information on guides, campgrounds and a good place to hang out with local sportsmen and pick up some tips.

The Dismal Swamp

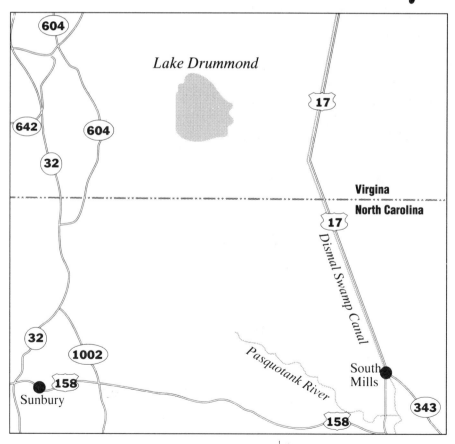

The Great Dismal Swamp National Wildlife Refuge is more than 100,000 acres of protected land in Virginia and North Carolina.

It's a three-mile paddle from Highway 17 to the heart of the Dismal. The Feeder Ditch branch of the Dismal Swamp Canal is a straight shot through thick woods, dead-ending at the dam and campground. A short portage and a few minutes of paddling reveals an opening in the dark forest, Lake Drummond. Cormorants stand guard on ancient cypress trees just offshore.

I drifted with the northeast wind, riding the waves and enjoying the music of crickets, bullfrogs and owls. For refreshment, I dipped a canteen cup into the lake and took a drink of unpolluted, golden water. The naturally acidic juniper water is supposed to be good for you. It was carried by old-time sailors on long voyages. Still tastes like swamp water to me. I suppose it's an acquired taste, like drinking beer – or exploring swamps.

The Dismal is not a depression in the ground like a typical swamp. It's more a low plateau, naturally flooded by the 3,100-acre Lake Drummond. In 1973, Union Camp Corp. donated 49,000 acres of the Dismal to the Nature Conservancy. This private conservation group turned it over to the U.S. Fish and Wildlife Service, and the Great Dismal Swamp National Wildlife Refuge was established in 1974. Today 107,000 acres in Virginia and North Carolina – less than half of the original swamp – are protected from logging and open for recreation.

The 166-square-mile preserve is roughly bounded by the city of Suffolk to the north, U.S. Highway 158 to the south, U.S. Highway 17 to the east, and N.C. Highway 32 to the west. The headquarters is off Virginia Highway 604 near the Railroad Ditch.

The ecology of this great swamp has been greatly altered by human activity. All of the swamp has been logged at least once. Ditches were dug to drain the wetlands. Red maples and loblolly pines – better suited to drier soil – have largely replaced the mature forest of cypress, gum and juniper that once stood here. In spite of all these changes, the swamp is still wild.

"We're trying to encourage the cypress and juniper to come back," said Teresa Cherry, the Outdoor Recreation Planner for the refuge.

Water conservation is one approach being used. Water control structures on the drainage ditches keep the swamp from drying out. It may be starting to work already. Young cypress trees are growing beside canals. Perhaps in a few hundred years, what remains of the great swamp forest will have returned to its original state.

A Nansemond Indian legend tells of Lake Drummond's creation. A "firebird" (possibly a meteor?) supposedly fell from the sky, leaving a big hole in the ground that eventually filled with water.

Modern theories of the swamp's creation speculate that an ancient wildfire could have burned this depression in the flammable peat of a huge bog, that beavers did the deed, or that the area was overwashed by the ocean long ago. Radio-carbon dating places the lake's age at 4,000 to 5,000 years.

Indians didn't remain long in the swamp's vicinity after the arrival of European settlers. The colonists avoided the swamp. Only hard-core hunters ventured into this unknown wilderness.

One such hunter was William Drummond, who discovered the lake that bears his name. He went into the swamp on a hunting expedition with a group of men and was the only one to return alive. He went on to become the first colonial governor of North Carolina from 1663 to 1667. His luck finally ran out in 1676 when he was hanged, drawn and quartered as a traitor for his part in Bacon's Rebellion. Nathaniel Bacon had defied orders from Governor Berkeley and organized a militia to fight hostile Indians. Drummond assisted in Bacon's efforts and was eventually captured and hung.

Col. William Byrd II gave a dismal account of the swamp when he surveyed the boundary between North Carolina and Virginia in 1728. " A very large swamp or bog...the foul Damps ascend without ceasing," he wrote in his *Historie of the Dividing Line Betwixt Virginia and North Carolina.* According to the colonel, a good supply of rum was the only way to endure this "vast body of dirt and nastiness" and "horrible desert."

This forested wetland between the Chesapeake Bay and Albemarle Sound was anything but a desert. The more enlightened – and sober – George Washington visited the swamp in 1763, called it a "glorious paradise" for wildlife, then started its destruction. A skilled surveyor, he was the first to figure out that the swamp was 20 feet above sea level – a depression on a ridge – and a cinch to drain. He took advantage of this discovery and invested in draining and logging operations. The timber rush began and continued for more than 200 years. Vast stands of virgin cypress and white cedar fell to the ax and cross-cut saw.

A five-mile-long canal and road to Lake Drummond – Washington Ditch – was constructed to get the timber out. This may be the first monument to bear the name of the Father of Our Country. A nearby stream was supposedly named by young Washington himself when he lost his footing, fell in and exclaimed, "Damn, that's a Deep Creek!" Yes, George Washington (forgive me) slipped here.

Washington and William Byrd agreed on the need for a canal

between Chesapeake Bay and Albemarle Sound for easier shipping and commerce. From 1793 to 1805, slave labor built a 22-mile-long ditch and road from Deep Creek to the Pasquotank River. A fleet of flatboats 30 to 40 feet long carried forest products and produce between North Carolina and Virginia along this waterway.

Runaway slaves often fled the work camps for the swamp, pursued by brutal bounty hunters and dogs. Many died, but the luckier ones escaped to a harsh freedom. Some built fortified settlements and traded with friends in town. Others lived as common criminals.

The notorious Halfway House Hotel served canal passengers and stagecoach travelers on the adjacent towpath – now U.S. Highway 17 – in the early 1800s. Impatient young couples from Virginia fled here to elope, taking advantage of lenient North Carolina marriage laws.

Lovers came for nights of forbidden passion, certain that they wouldn't be discovered in this out-of-the-way inn. Men of honor dueled here and settled disputes – usually over a woman – with a pistol or sword. Outlaws liked the hotel because it straddled the state line, offering them the opportunity to avoid arrest. When a lawman from either state showed up, the fugitive just stepped to the other side of the building and out of the officer's jurisdiction. There was another hotel on Lake Drummond with an even worse reputation, described as a "place of tawdry entertainment and frequented by boisterous and rowdy types."

If some people came to the swamp for nefarious purposes, the swamp attracted those with higher callings as well. Poets sought inspiration here. Edgar Allen Poe is said to have penned his gloomy epic, "The Raven," during a visit to the swamp. Thomas Moore of Ireland composed "The Lake of the Dismal Swamp" based on Indian tales of mysterious nocturnal lights – supposedly the spirits of Indian lovers who perished in the lake but were re-united forever in death.

Moore wrote:

But oft, from the Indian hunter's camp,
  This lover and maid so true
Are seen at the hour of midnight damp
To cross the Lake by a fire-fly lamp,
  And paddle their white canoe!

Strange lights are still seen in the swamp at night. Some folks insist they're ghosts or UFOs. Official explanations point to the glowing patches of phosphorus found on trees – called foxfire or swamp gas. Either way, those shimmers in the night put on a spooky show.

The swamp's macabre reputation probably was the reason that Robert Frost came here to kill himself after being spurned by a woman he loved. Happily, he changed his mind and traveled on to the Outer Banks. Refreshed by his travels, he returned to Boston, won the woman's hand and went on to become poet laureate of America.

During the War of 1812, the British Navy controlled the open sea and the canal that George Washington conceived became an important supply route for the American forces. The waterway was enlarged at this time and a 20-ton vessel made the passage in 1814. Confederate forces shipped supplies through this protected waterway until 1863, thus averting the Union blockade during the Civil War. A Union officer stationed in the area wrote in 1864, "We were in the dreariest part of the Dismal Swamp. The darkness was dense, the ghastly silence broken only by the hooting of owls and the crying of wildcats."

Logging continued in the swamp. More than 140 miles of logging roads were built with their associated drainage ditches. Narrow-gauge railroads were constructed for hauling the timber to market. As land continued to be drained and cleared, farms were carved out of the wilderness.

Melvin Brinkley's father started the first tobacco farm on the northwestern border of the present refuge, moving here from Colerain, North Carolina, when Melvin just was seven years old. Melvin grew up an enthusiastic outdoorsman, hunting deer, raccoons and bears all over the Dismal. Today, the retired farmer and shipyard worker still lives on the well-tended family farm. A hip fracture and a stroke have slowed him, but he still likes to tell of his most memorable bear hunt back in the '30s.

One afternoon when Melvin was feeding the hogs and saw a big bear lurking in a field, he got his gun and shot it. "I knew I hit him, because I found a blood trail," he said. He tried to track the bear through the swamp, but darkness soon descended and Melvin went back to the house for a lantern and his favorite 'coon dog.

"That dog got one whiff and ran back under the house, his tail between his legs," he said. "He won't having nothing to do with no bear."

Melvin took a compass bearing and marked the bear's line of travel, then went home to sleep. But he returned at first light to resume the search. He struggled for hours through a thick tangle of briars and brambles that restricted visibility to a few feet, then stepped onto a rise to get a better look. But something told him to look down. "I was standing on the bear!" he said.

Melvin Brinkley has lived on the outskirts of the Dismal Swamp since he was seven years old. In the 1930s, he killed a bear in the swamp, and had the head mounted.

Fortunately for Melvin, the critter was already dead. Melvin and his family ate that 350-pound bear, but the head was mounted and is still proudly displayed.

Melvin's plows have unearthed more trophies over the years – arrowheads, spearpoints, knives and axes – all carved from stone by ancient hands. Stone is not found in this area, but the Indians of the coastal plain were known to trade with tribes in the western part of the state where stone was common.

Melvin's family used to have a cabin on Lake Drummond, where they could always catch a mess of catfish. "The U.S. Fish and Wildlife Service burnt that cabin down when the refuge came in," he said.

He's still sore about it. He used to ride a horse and buggy to the lake every Saturday until a few years ago. "Now they say the only way you can get to the lake is to walk or ride a bicycle," he said. "How am I supposed to walk out there or ride a bicycle with a broken hip?"

Still, Melvin agrees that the refuge probably is a good thing. He admits life wouldn't be the same without the Dismal in his back yard.

It's only 12 miles from his property line east to Highway 17, but

Cormorants
can be found
in the cypress
trees in Lake
Drummond.

those are precious miles as far as bears are concerned. A 1988 survey showed that some 400 bears called that swampy area home. The black bear is the symbol of the refuge now – adorning its signs and brochures – but few visitors are lucky to see one. Bear tracks are fairly easy to find, however.

Bears are hunted on private property that surrounds the refuge but no bear hunting is allowed in the refuge. Limited hunting keeps the plentiful deer from overgrazing the refuge. A record number of deer, 396, were taken in 1991. The deer hunting season is from October 1 through November 30, with hunting allowed only on Thursdays, Fridays and Saturdays. Hunters must have valid licenses and acquire permits from the refuge headquarters. They also should check in at headquarters before hunting.

The refuge has an elaborate trail system that is popular with joggers, hikers and bicyclists. Free maps are available at the headquarters, where current trail conditions are posted.

The most popular trail is the Washington Ditch from White Marsh Road to Lake Drummond. This former logging path is 4.5 miles long, level and well marked, open to bicyclists and hikers. At the head of this trail is the Boardwalk Trail, a one-mile loop through the swamp forest that is open only to hikers.

The rest of the trail system is made up of old logging roads that run straight through the woods, allowing plenty of room to wander. Deer often are seen on the trails. Otters, nutria, turtles, wood ducks and great blue herons are plentiful in the overgrown canals.

Bird watching is popular in the Dismal. More than 200 species have been identified and 93 are known to nest here. Spring brings migrations of warblers and songbirds, including the rare Swanson's warbler and Wayne's warbler, both of which are abundant in the swamp. Winter is noted for the large numbers of assorted blackbirds and robins that return each year. One study recorded the blackbird count at more than 50 million. Owls hoot and woodpeckers tap all over the swamp. Cormorants and a few osprey are occasionally seen in Lake Drummond.

The Dismal is the northern limit for many southern plants and animals: bald-cypress, Spanish moss and the dreaded water moccasin are just a few. This is the first link in the chain of southern coastal swamps that stretches all the way to Florida's Everglades.

Five types of forest communities are found on the refuge. Red maple is the most common followed by pine. The North Carolina portion of the refuge protects a 75-acre virgin stand of rare Atlantic white cedar (juniper) near the Corapeake Ditch. Tupelo gum and bald cypress are found in wet, swampy regions. Upland hardwoods such as oak, poplar and sweetgum inhabit the drier areas. Marshes, bogs, pocosins and grassy areas that are locally called "lights" make up the rest of the refuge.

Rare plants found in the swamp include the dwarf trillium, which only blooms for a couple of weeks in March. The plant grows only three or four inches high. The blossoms usually are purple but pink and white also are seen. Wild camellias grow to 15 feet on hardwood ridges and start blooming in late May. Both the trillium and camellias can be found in the northwestern part of the refuge near the Jericho Ditch. At least 173 different trees, shrubs, vines, ferns and flowers grow here – enough to keep the avid botanist happy for a while.

Of the 38 mammal species living in the swamp, the black bear is the largest and most rarely seen. Hikers should have no trouble spotting deer. Bobcats are often heard but seldom seen. Grey foxes, opossums, raccoons, squirrels, rabbits, bats, mice and shrews are common. Minks, otters, muskrats and nutria live in the canals, creeks and rivers. Panthers and wolves were hunted and trapped out of existence long ago.

The swamp crawls with snakes, including cottonmouths, copperheads and canebrake rattlers, plus 18 non-venomous species. Fifty-six

species of turtles, lizards, salamanders, frogs and toads have been identified in the swamp. Colonel William Byrd II reported seeing alligators
here in 1728, but none are known to remain.

Billions of biting insects make up for any lack of other voracious
creatures. The warmer the weather, the more active – and hungry – the
insects get. Plenty of repellent is required to keep them at bay.

"We preserve and protect a unique habitat," Teresa Cherry said of
the refuge she manages. "It's a quiet area where people can get out and
enjoy nature." Her staff will provide an orientation briefing if notified
in advance.

Sometimes certain roads in the refuge will be closed, usually to protect an endangered species that can't tolerate human activity. Most
enforcement officers will simply ask you to leave if you wander into
these areas, but they can and do arrest deliberate violators. Rules are
listed on the official maps and pamphlets available at headquarters and
the visitor center.

There's only one campground in the Dismal, the Lake Drummond
Reservation, which is operated by the Army Corps of Engineers. It's
only three miles from U.S. 17, but the only way to reach it is by a small
boat drawing four feet of water or less. Excellent docks are provided.
The campground is on a peninsula between the canal and lake and is
equipped with grills, a dozen picnic tables, two screened shelters and
restrooms with running water. The water is shut off from December
until March. Camping is free; just sign in and keep the place clean. The
campground is especially popular with canoeists.

The campground sits next to the dam that controls water going out
of Lake Drummond. A locked chain-link gate and fence separate the
campground from the buildings used for dam operations. A short
marine railway can portage boats weighing 1,000 pounds or less from
the Feeder Ditch to the lake. An attendant is on duty seven days a week
from 8:00 a.m. to 4:00 p.m. but the portage railway can be operated by
boaters after hours. Just place the boat on the cradle and push the but-
ton. Only outboard motors up to 10 horsepower are allowed in the shallow lake, which is only six feet at the deepest point. This lake can get
rough quickly when the wind is up – some say it's worse than the
Chesapeake Bay – so mind the weather.

Earl Dale is in charge of the Lake Drummond Reservation. He
grew up in nearby South Mills and has worked for the Corps of Engineers for more than 25 years.

"We've had as many as fifty boats on the lake some days," he said.
"Other times, there won't be a single boat out there."

April and May are the busiest times. Lots of citation-size black crappie are caught at that time of the year. Small catfish and assorted panfish bite year-round. Attempts to stock largemouth bass in the lake didn't work out because of the heavy concentrations of tannic acid in the water.

At one time, campers at the reservation had to be concerned about bears, according to Earl. Some local people had raised bear cubs as pets until they got too big to keep, then released them into the swamp. Those bears, accustomed to getting food from people, would show up at the campground hoping to be fed, and frightening campers. All of them had to be rounded up and relocated. Now campers don't have to worry much about bears, but raccoons do occasionally raid the campground's trash cans.

Campers should be concerned about snakes, though, says Earl. "Even if you don't see them, they're around all right."

Yet, he could only recall one snake bite in all of his years at the reservation. A young boy riding a bicycle ran over a small copperhead, fell down and was bitten when he picked up his bike. He recovered without difficulty.

The Dismal Swamp Canal is the oldest operating artificial waterway in the United States. It's listed in the National Register of Historic Places and is designated a National Historic Civil Engineering Landmark. It is an alternate route of the Atlantic Intracoastal Waterway, but boaters must pass through two sets of locks, one at South Mills, North Carolina, the other at Deep Creek, Virginia. A visitors center has been built alongside the canal five miles north of the South Mills locks to serve boaters and motorists on U.S. Highway 17. The center has a 150-foot dock for boaters and plenty of parking space for wheeled vehicles. There is a large picnic ground. The center's staff provides maps, brochures and other information about area attractions. An excellent videotape about the swamp will be shown upon request.

The once-dreaded and nearly destroyed Dismal is now an island of recovering wilderness in a rapidly developing area. Within easy reach of nearby Tidewater, Virginia, it offers escape, breath-taking beauty, intrigue and adventure. And there's nothing dismal about that.

For more information about the Dismal Swamp:

Great Dismal Swamp National Wildlife Refuge
PO Box 349
Suffolk, Va. 23434-034
(804) 986-3705
Open Monday-Friday 7:00 a.m. to 3:30 p.m. Closed on holidays. Maps, brochures and up-to-date trail conditions available. Tours and orientation briefings can be arranged with two weeks notice. Open house usually is held in September.

Chesapeake Campgrounds
693 South George Washington Highway
Chesapeake, Va.
(804) 485-5686
Located across Highway 17 from Dismal Swamp Canal. Campsites for RV's and tents. Canoe rentals available, reservations suggested.

Dismal Swamp Canal Visitor Center
Route 1, Box 149
South Mills, N.C. 27976
(919) 771-8333
Cruising boaters can call for current lock schedules and canal water levels.

U.S, Army Corps of Engineers
Norfolk District Office
903 Front Street
Norfolk, Va. 23510-1096
Can provide maps and current navigation conditions on the Dismal Swamp and Albemarle & Chesapeake Canal.
(804)-441-7606

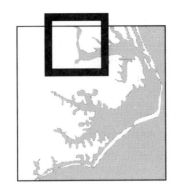

The Chowan River

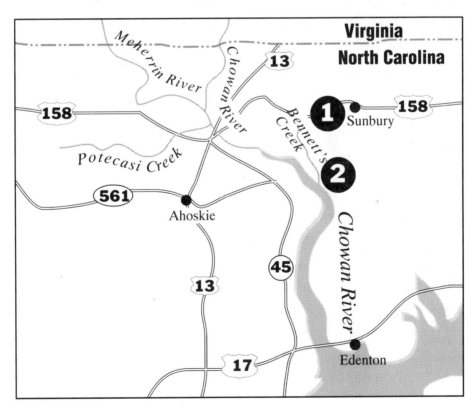

1. Merchants Millpond State Park
2. Chowan Swamp Canoe Trail and
   Game Lands

Earl Pierce, chief of the 565-member Meherrin Indian tribe, enjoys fishing on the Potecasi Creek.

Otters frolicked in the black water at sunset. My little boat drifted silently with the wind, getting ever closer. Finally the otters fled, kicking up warning splashes with their hind legs as they left, except for one bold youngster that swam right in my direction. Just 20 feet away, he turned, his sleek back glistening, and escorted me through his territory to the mouth of the Meherrin River. I welcomed the company as we floated along together past the site of an old Indian village. Then a splash and the otter was gone, leaving me to paddle the Chowan River alone.

The Chowan is fed by swampy tributaries such as the Meherrin and an old Indian canoe trail now called Bennett's Creek as it flows southward from the Virginia line for nearly 50 peaceful miles to the Albemarle Sound. Peaceful though it may appear, the Chowan valley has a long history of human conflict that continues today, as the newly reorganized Meherrin Indian Tribe attempts to regain tribal lands.

An Iroquois tribe called the Chowanooks named this river and lived here long before the first Englishman, Ralph Lane, visited during a 1586 expedition from the ill-fated Roanoke Island Colony. He visited the Indian communities and raided their fishtraps. He went on to start the first war between the English and the Indians, thus beginning the destruction of a civilization.

Later, other English settlers were drawn to the Chowan, coming southward from Virginia, following a well traveled Indian canoe trail from the Great Dismal Swamp to Albemarle Sound that took them along Bennett's Creek to the river. The creek was named for the first Englishman to explore the stream, Richard Bennett, Governor of Virginia from 1652 until 1655.

William Edmundson, a soldier turned missionary, followed Bennett's Creek to the Chowan in the spring of 1672. He wrote in his journal, "It being upon me, I traveled to Carolina...it being all wilderness, and no English inhabitants or pathways, but some marked trees to guide people." He returned that fall with George Fox, founder of the Society of Friends, better known as Quakers. These simple, devout people earned their nickname because they were said to "quake" with religious fervor. These gentle pioneers held the first formal religious services in the Carolina Colony, an event now commemorated by a granite memorial beside the Perquimans River at Hertford. George Fox also preached to the Indians and was impressed by their moral values and belief in a higher power. Fox and most other Quakers treated the Indians with respect.

But other settlers did not and war came to the Chowan three years after Fox's arrival. The Chowanooks were driven into the swamps around Bennett's Creek where they operated as a guerrilla force. For years the Indians were said to haunt the woods, and travel here was risky.

About that time the Meherrin Tribe was driven out of Virginia along the Chowan tributary that bears their name. Related to the other Iroquois tribes – the Tuscarora, Cherokee, Chowanooks and Machapunga – the Meherrin were known as the phantom tribe because of their reputation for stealth.

"We would rather count coup on an enemy than kill him," said Earl Pierce, chief of the newly resurrected Meherrin Tribe. Warriors, he explained, liked to sneak into an enemy camp and leave a feather or arrow close to an unsuspecting victim, then depart unseen – an act of high honor. "When my enemy wakes up and sees that I spared his life, he knows his life belongs to me," said Earl. "I can take it from him any time." Disputes were sometimes settled this way without bloodshed.

The invading white settlers played for keeps, however, especially after the brutal massacres of the Tuscarora wars of 1711-1713. The Meherrin ran guns to the Tuscarora at first, then switched sides, capturing the leaders of the rebellion and turning them over to the whites. In 1729, the Meherrin were granted a three-square-mile reservation where the Chowan and Meherrin Rivers meet. Attacks by Seneca war parties, a yellow fever epidemic and harassment by the whites eventually drove the Meherrin off the reservation. The Meherrin had to disperse and adopt the white man's ways and language to survive. Meherrin families took English names. Members of other tribes settled among them. Eventually, there were marriages between Indians, whites and blacks.

More trouble came to the Chowan when the Civil War broke out. Winton was the first town in North Carolina to be torched and looted by Union troops. Bands of military deserters from both sides terrorized the lawless countryside. In 1864, conditions got so bad that Union and Confederate cavalry units mounted joint operations to subdue these roving bands of cutthroats.

After the war, peace once again returned to the river. People lived quiet lives along the river and its tributaries, farming, fishing, logging. With time, many would begin commuting to jobs in shipyards and factories in the cities of Tidewater Virginia.

Signs along the river now warn about eating fish caught from these waters. They have been contaminated by a paper mill in Virginia. Still there are tributaries that lead to swamps where the water is fresh and clear and the fish are free of poisons. One such is Potecasi Creek.

"It's good to be home," said Earl Pierce, who works as a house painter and preaches in Baptist churches. We'd just scrambled and slid down a slippery embankment to reach the swampy blackwater creek. It was too overgrown for a canoe. Mosquitoes flocked around us, waiting for our sweat to wash off the bug spray that kept them at bay. Cypress and gum trees blocked the September sun.

"Watch where you walk," Earl said. "There's just enough snakes around here to keep it interesting." He told of being bitten on the ear by a cottonmouth on the first day of squirrel season years ago. It almost killed him. For years afterward he sought revenge, killing every snake he saw, until a wise old shaman pointed out the folly of punishing all snakes because one cottonmouth did him wrong. He reminded Earl that the Creator put everything on earth for a purpose, even snakes.

Earl said that he went back into the forest to fast and meditate on this. While there he encountered a huge diamondback rattler – the most dangerous snake in North America. He talked to the snake, he said, and it stopped its threatening rattling and allowed him to approach and dance around it. Earl made his peace with snakes and life that day, restoring harmony to his soul. It allowed him to assume his role as hereditary chief of the 565 member Meherrin Tribe. Still he keeps an eye out for snakes.

We hiked through boot-sucking mud along the creek's edge, staying out of the swamp grass and ferns, stopping occasionally to identify and gather medicinal plants, coonface for burns, heart leaf for congestion. Along the shore a few inches of mud hid a rare blue clay prized by Indian potters, and Earl stooped to expose it. Freshwater springs flowed to the banks, offering refreshment. Mussels crowded the creek bottom, food for raccoons and other creatures. We shook wild grapes from vines twining high into the trees and sucked their sweet juices.

We crossed the creek on a massive cypress tree that had blown down. It could make a dugout big enough to carry a dozen men. Finally, we reached an open stretch of creek bank.

Earl cast three times and caught three fish – two robins and a bass – in about two minutes. He used a spinning reel with an artificial lure, a red rooster tail spinner, but he spoke of the old times, when his people hunted and fished with spears and bows. The Meherrin constructed fish traps from strips of wood to funnel the fish into small areas where they could be speared easily. Herring ran up the creek every spring, so thick, said Earl, that a person almost could walk on them. The Meherrin caught them in nets made from hemp and preserved them by smoking and drying.

Earl spoke of a lifetime on this land and the lives of his ancestors who had lived here before him. He had found his ancestors' bones by feeling their energy radiating from the ground, he said. The Meherrin are attempting to document their rightful claim to this land with extensive genealogical research. The tribe won state recognition in 1977 and is hoping to achieve federal recognition soon. With Federal recognition they hope to regain at least some of the reservation that was granted them back in 1729.

If they regain the three-mile circle of land currently owned by a timber company and private citizens, the Meherrin hope to support themselves on it by farming, fishing, hunting and welcoming visitors. Their plans include building campgrounds and marinas, hiking and canoe trails, and opening the reservation to recreational use. Meherrin guides would take visitors through the forest to observe nature the Indian way, in harmony with the wilderness. The Meherrins have a "land fund," and are slowly buying small parcels of land for the tribe.

Merchants Millpond State Park

All North Carolinians own some land in the Chowan valley. At Merchants Millpond State Park just off U.S. Highway 158 in Gates County, the state holds title to 2,659 acres, all of it open to public use. The main attraction at the park is the 760-acre millpond that was created when Bennett's Creek was dammed to power a grist mill in 1812. Folks used to come here to get their corn ground. Now some 80,000 visitors come each year to get away from the grind of modern life.

The park offers canoe trails, hiking paths and campsites for RVs and tents. Those who don't like crowded campgrounds can hike or paddle to more isolated sites. Canoes can be rented to explore the millpond and Lassiter's Swamp. The swamp is a remnant of the great swamp forests that once dominated northeastern North Carolina. Hunting isn't allowed in the park but Bennett's Creek flows into the Chowan Swamp Game Lands on the shore of the Chowan River, where the bottomlands are full of deer and bears. Fishing is allowed in the park and largemouth bass, crappie, bream and pickerel are abundant.

"We think we have the best park anywhere," said Dennis Helms, park superintendent. "We aim to keep it that way. We are fortunate. Our visitors are serious outdoor people that really appreciate the natural beauty here. They pack out their trash and help take care of the place."

Kitchen Norfleet built the dam and the original mill here. Water

Lassiter's Swamp in Merchants Millpond State Park.

A turtle makes his way through Merchants Millpond State Park.

power ground corn, milled wheat and sawed timber. A mercantile store was built and the mill complex became the commercial center of Gates County. Locals dubbed this 19th century shopping center Merchants Millpond.

People shopped, fished and partied while getting their grinding and milling done. The mill operated until just before World War II. After it closed this once thriving center of commerce fell into ruin, neglected by all but a few people who came to the pond to fish.

Then a retired sailor turned land developer, the late A.B. Coleman, discovered Lassiter's Swamp and the millpond during a canoe trip down Bennett's Creek.

Coleman was an outdoorsman and avid paddler who'd journeyed to wilderness areas all over the country. He thought the millpond was the most beautiful place he'd ever seen and was determined to own it. He bought the property in 1968 and began showing it off to visitors. He could have made a nice sum developing the land, but he decided it was just too special for that. In 1973 he donated the millpond and surrounding land to the state to be used as a park.

"You got to do things for reasons other than money if you're going to accomplish anything in life," he once said in an interview with *Wildlife in North Carolina*. Later that year the Nature Conservancy added another 925 acres to the park. Additional purchases by the state expanded the park to its present size.

Coleman's legacy, in modern terms, might be called a user friendly swamp. Each season has its own delights. Spring brings out the songbirds. By summer insects and turtles are all over the place. Great blue herons stalk the shallows. Barred owls hunt for frogs, fish and rodents. Ticks lurk in the undergrowth, waiting to feed on those who don't take precautions against them. In warm weather the black water of the pond and swamp often appears smeared with green because of the duckweed that thrives on the fertilizer runoff from upstream farms. Cold weather and good rains thin out the scummy stuff. Winter drives the bugs, snakes and duckweed away and brings more than 2,000 wintering ducks, including the exotic hooded mergansers.

Fishing is a major attraction here in all seasons. Several largemouth bass in the seven- to eight-pound range are taken every summer, according to ranger Floyd Williams. Crappie bite voraciously in the winter. Tasty bluegills and hard-fighting jack (pickerel) are caught through much of the year. Nearby stores offer licenses, bait, tackle and advice. Gasoline motors are forbidden on the park waters. Only boats powered by paddles or electric trolling motors are allowed.

Hikers can spot deer at dawn on the 6.2-mile trail on the north bank of the millpond. The trail is well marked and maintained by scout groups and volunteers. Foot bridges span the boggy places. Most of the trail is an easy walk on dry ground through stands of beech, maple and pine. Maps are available at the ranger station. Check for ticks during and after the hike in warm weather.

Rent a canoe and paddle waters once traveled by warriors, missionaries and pioneers. Marvel at the living swamp forest that glides by with every paddle stroke. Penetrate Lassiter's Swamp – if you dare to enter the Enchanted Forest. Not many people do. Here you can experience one of the last old growth swamp forests. Some of the cypress trees here are thought to be 1,000 years old. Some are eight feet in diameter and nearly 120 feet tall. The tupelo gum trees here are the tallest in the state. Mistletoe infests their upper branches and the trees have developed strange woody growths to cover the parasites. Resurrection ferns cling to these ancient, moss-cloaked giants.

Beavers have returned to the swamp after being trapped out in the '30s. One beaver dam is more than 2,000 feet long.

The wild song of insects and amphibians is a constant drone in the summer swamp. When the frogs get tuned up the very air vibrates. The air is thick with the odor of new life and decay – eau de swamp. There is no clearly defined channel through these spooky woods. Newcomers are advised to stay near the edges at first. It's easy to get disoriented. Experience, a compass and a good sense of direction are necessary to explore the depths of the swamp, a worthy challenge for any wilderness traveler.

Campers at Merchants Millpond have three options. The main campground has 20 drive-in sites for tents and RV's (no hook-ups). Each site has a lantern stand, fireplace, picnic table, tent pad, and plenty of shade. This is a standard state park campground arranged around a paved loop road that encircles a central bathhouse (with the luxury of hot showers). The campground is neat and orderly. Dead wood can be gathered for campfires. Every time I've used this campground, previous campers had left enough wood for a fire – a courtesy that's encouraged. One disadvantage of this campground is that you have to put up with the noise of Highway 158 just a few hundred yards away.

Backpack campers can swap modern conveniences for peace and quiet at five primitive campgrounds removed from the highway. Owls and whippoorwills sound a lot better at night than Macks and Peterbilts. If you choose this option, you must bring everything you need, including drinking water.

Paddling a canoe in Merchants Millpond State Park.

The canoe camps are the deluxe suites in this outdoor inn. Paddlers just follow the colored buoys from the landing to their luxuriously primitive accommodations, complete with pit toilets. Follow the orange buoys to the seven sites at the family canoe camp less than a mile away. Yellow markers lead a little deeper into the swamp to the three group canoe camps. For a real adventure, paddle the swamp after dark and catch the nocturnal wildlife action. Take a good flashlight and plenty of batteries.

Chowan Swamp Canoe Trail and Game Lands

Bennett's Creek is designated the Chowan Swamp Canoe Trail downstream from the park. You can't take the state park canoes down this trail, so you'll need to bring your own boat. It's 14 miles of meandering black water to the wide and powerful Chowan River. The stretch between the park and the N.C. Highway 37 bridge is narrow and shallow with plenty of beaver dams to drag canoes over. Most paddlers put in at the bridge. Primitive camping is available on Hermit's Island, about a mile downstream from the bridge. Bears travel this wilderness highway between the Dismal and Chowan Swamps. If you're quiet and lucky, you might see one.

Be ready for windy, big-water paddling on the Chowan. Most people ride the current and take out at the State Wildlife Commission boat landing at Cannon's Ferry.

Just upstream from the mouth of Bennett's Creek is another branch of the Chowan trail, Sareem Creek, that leads to Taylor's Millpond. Winter and early spring offer the best water conditions to paddle this trail. Spring and summer bring low water, bugs and snakes. This stream is for dedicated wilderness explorers.

The state Department of Natural and Economic Resources owns 6,959 acres in four tracts along the Chowan. Stretches of old growth cypress and gum can be found along the marshes and creeks along with bottomland hardwood forest. This area is managed by the N.C. Wildlife Resources Commission for hunting. Good waterfowl potential. Deer hunting described as average, and there are no turkeys in this swamp. Hunting for squirrels and marsh rabbits is excellent.

Chowan Game Land is a 30-acre plot bordering U.S. Highway 17. It's all a thick gum swamp and few people use it. Wildlife watchers can observe the plentiful wading birds and waterfowl just by pulling off the highway and walking a sort distance.

The Chowan River valley still offers adventure, as it has since humans first penetrated it. Beginning explorers can get a taste of the swamp paddling at Merchants Millpond, then take on the wilder areas as they gain skill and nerve. More experienced prowlers can find all the challenge, isolation and wildness they want.

For more information about the Chowan area:

Merchants Millpond State Park
Route 1 Box 141-A
Gatesville, N.C. 27938
(919) 357-1191
Call for schedule of activities and campsite reservations.

Meherrin Indian Tribe
PO Box 508
Winton, N.C. 27980
(919) 358-4375
Annual pow-wow in October open to the public. Indian arts and crafts for sale at the tribal office.

Chowan Swamp canoe trail information:
Cypress Group of the Sierra Club
1908 Forest Hill Dr.
Greenville, N.C. 27834

Carolina Wilderness Institute
126 East Fisher Ave.
Greensboro, N.C. 27401
(919) 274-1033

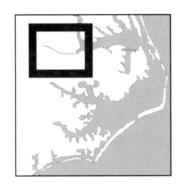

The Roanoke River

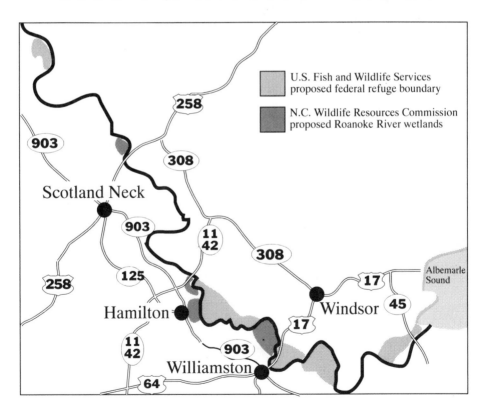

U.S. Fish and Wildlife Services proposed federal refuge boundary

N.C. Wildlife Resources Commission proposed Roanoke River wetlands

258

903

308

Scotland Neck

903

11
42

308

258

125

17

Albemarle
Sound

Hamilton

Windsor

45

17

11
42

903

Williamston

64

A fisherman on the Roanoke River gets a strike.

The Indians named it Moratuck. Some have called it the River of Death because of its swift currents and tendencies to flood. Floods used to wipe out entire Indian villages along its banks.

The water was fast and muddy as it raced from the Blue Ridge Mountains of Virginia toward Albemarle Sound, 400 miles from its headwaters. I watched from a landing in Bertie County at a place known as Indian Woods, once the site of a Tuscarora Indian reservation. Whirlpools came and went. Logs floated by just below the surface, propelled through the current like torpedoes. Spring flood stage is not the time to paddle the Roanoke River alone. The canoe stayed on the rack.

I went fishing instead with Marvin Williamson and his son Marvin Jr. They own a tobacco farm at Old Ford and bring their boat to the river every spring for the herring run.

Marvin ran the boat upstream from the landing in Jamesville, toward the long, dark bend in an area called the Devils Gut. He turned the boat around and switched off the outboard. We were adrift in the swift current. The cypress and gum trees on the banks rushed by.

Marvin had hurt his hand the week before, so his son would have to work the net today. "Usually he works the nets and I drive the boat," said the younger Marvin, a little anxiously. "This is the first time I've worked the net by myself."

He threw the net over the side like a pro and the floats snaked across the brown water. Boat and net drifted downstream, caught in the river's power. Once something slammed the hull but the fiberglass held.

Soon the cork floats trembled and bobbed in the muddy water. The gill net was heavy with fish and the apprentice fisherman hauled it in. Only 14, he was lean and strong from working on the farm. With a big grin on his face, he picked the fish from the net and packed them in the cooler.

Each year these sleek fish return from the ocean, swimming into the swift current, running a gantlet of predators. The stronger and luckier fish make it to their ancient spawning grounds and a new generation begins. The rest end up as dinner.

Marvin's face glowed with quiet pride as he watched his son fish. Yet there was a sadness in his eyes. "I just hope he can bring his son here one day," he said. "But by the time he's grown, there may not be any herring left."

Older fishermen tell of catching more herring than their boats could

Marvin Williamson, right, and son Marvin Jr., below, use nets to fish for herring on the Roanoke River.

carry. On spring weekends, the banks were lined with fishermen using large homemade nets. Some fish were cleaned, cooked and eaten right on the riverbank, the rest corned – preserved in salt and corn meal. Families shared the feast and festivities. The river fed its followers.

Foreign fishing fleets and declining water quality have hurt the traditional herring fishery in recent years. But now the herring are getting a break. Part of their spawning grounds are being protected from further development and pollution by a new wildlife refuge along the Roanoke.

The Roanoke River basin drains more than 10,000 square miles, 3,500 miles of it east of the fall line that separates the Coastal Plain from the Piedmont Plateau. Along the 137-mile stretch of the river in North Carolina, the floodplain is five miles wide in places. Brown, nutrient-rich water occasionally rises over the natural levees and floods the fields and forests behind them, sometimes creating backswamps. Early planters made fortunes from the rich bottomlands, and farming is still a major occupation along the river's banks.

From the time humans first encountered the river, it has served as a highway. The arrival of white settlers and the commerce they generated made the river even more important. The towns of Williamston and Plymouth developed into busy ports. At one point, 23 different steamboat companies ran goods and passengers up and down the river.

That made the river of vital strategic interest when the Civil War erupted. Union and Confederate troops battled for control of the Roanoke. The rebels built a complex of earthworks near Hamilton atop the 100-foot-high clay bluffs known as Rainbow Banks to protect the railroad bridge at Weldon. This railroad connected the port at Wilmington with the Confederate capitol of Richmond, a critical supply route. Fort Branch, named for a fallen Confederate general, Lawrence O'Brian Branch, had 12 cannons and a commanding view of the river.

With protection from the fort, Confederate forces were able to prepare an attack on the Union-held town of Plymouth with a secret weapon upstream – an ironclad ship, the C.S.S. Albemarle. In April of 1864, the Albemarle sailed toward Plymouth with the spring flood, sank the U.S.S. Southfield, killing her commander, and chased the U.S.S. Miami off the river. Troops from North Carolina, Georgia and Virginia liberated the town in three days, the last Confederate victory of the war.

Only seven months later, the Albemarle was blown up at the dock by a daring Federal commando team in a small boat. With the Albemarle gone, Federal gunboats again controlled the river below Fort Branch. The Union Army captured Plymouth four days later but Fort Branch held out to the end. When General Lee surrendered to Grant on April 10, 1965 at Appomattox, the fort was abandoned and its guns dumped into the river to keep them out of enemy hands.

Eight of those cannons have been recovered and are displayed on weekends at the fort, which still offers visitors a commanding view of the river. A re-enactment of the great battle is held each November at the fort, complete with the crack of musketry and the thunder of cavalry and artillery. Local volunteers work hard to honor the memory of the brave men on both sides.

After the war, the river remained an important transportation route until about the 1920s, when highway vehicles put the steamboats out of business. Barges filled with logs still cruise the Roanoke, but most of the river traffic today is made up of hunters, fishers, pleasure boaters and people who like to observe nature.

Today, the river is harnessed and controlled upstream. Just after World War II a flood washed through the valley of the Roanoke, causing great loss of life and property. In the early 1950s the U.S. Army Corps of Engineers constructed a series of dams near the Virginia line to control flooding and generate electricity. The dams disrupted the reproductive cycles of striped bass that migrated upriver to spawn. Many were trapped behind the dams, unable to return to the sea.

These fish can't spawn in most lakes, because their eggs need a steady flow of water to keep them suspended for at least 72 hours. In 1988, the water release from the upstream dam was carefully regulated to produce favorable spawning conditions downstream. It worked, providing hope that the striped bass population could recover.

That and more restrictive limits are gradually restoring the fishery. Anglers at the first rapids in Weldon report the fishing has greatly improved. The fish are so thick during the spring run that fishermen hit them with boat propellers at times. Wildlife officials monitor the fishing and cut the season off when a certain quota is reached. In 1991 the season lasted 19 days. But you can catch and release all you want.

Fishing conditions are less than desirable downstream from the huge paper mill near Plymouth that fouls the air and water. Signs along the river warn against eating fish because of dioxin contamination. But the paper mill supposedly is converting to a system of bleaching paper that will release no dioxin.

Still there is another threat to the river. The fast growing city of Virginia Beach wants to pump 60 million gallons of water each day out of Lake Gaston through a 90-mile pipeline to spur new development. Among causing other problems, this will harm the striped bass and herring runs. The two states are squabbling over rights to the water and the problem will have to be resolved in federal court.

Meanwhile the river flows with water of exceptional quality and its wetlands are known nationally as the best stretch of bottomland swamp forest left on the Mid-Atlantic coast. Undisturbed wetlands filter pollutants, control flood levels, and provide habitat for wildlife and recreation for people. In 1989 the Roanoke River National Wildlife Refuge was established to protect this rare habitat in Bertie, Halifax and Martin counties.

The Migratory Bird Conservation Fund, funded by Duck Stamp sales to waterfowl hunters eventually will pay for 33,000 acres of land on four tracts along the river between Weldon and Plymouth. The North Carolina Wildlife Resources Commission will manage 14,000 acres for public hunting and camping on the south side of the river.

Headquarters for this refuge is in a borrowed office at the Bertie County Courthouse in Windsor. The first staff member hired was the manager, Jerry Holliman, who was born and reared about 50 miles northwest of Windsor, in Northhampton county, where he fished the Roanoke as a boy. He started his career with a summer job at the refuge on Pea Island in 1967 while earning degrees in wildlife science and animal ecology from N.C. State University. He's worked all over the south with the U.S. Fish and Wildlife Service. Now he's making this refuge a reality.

"I want everybody who lives along the Roanoke to feel like they're stockholders in the river," he said. "The fishermen already feel that way."

At this writing, 6,200 acres of the allotted 33,000 acres had been purchased. The acquisition process is slow. The Fish & Wildlife Service, seeking community support, isn't pressuring anyone to sell land.

Holliman wants a new visitors center to be the hub of a network of self-guided interpretive trails, including boardwalks through the wet sections. Visitors could learn the importance and the wonders of the forested wetlands.

"This particular refuge is going to have, we think, some unique opportunities for canoe trails," he said. "Also, and I prefer not to use the standard term hiking trail, but trails for bird watchers and people who are serious about wildlife observation. It's muddy and the insects are horrible in the summer. I don't think people that hike just for hiking's sake will be interested."

Holliman has big dreams for the refuge. He wants to establish a major fresh water aquarium beside the river and set up the fish hatchery at Weldon – one of the world's oldest – as attractions for visitors. Local businesses could serve the developing tourist industry. He's won the enthusiastic support of the governments and citizens of Bertie and Halifax Counties.

It's a different story across the river. Martin County commissioners opposed the refuge. Hunting clubs have leased land from timber companies along the river in Martin County for generations. Club members didn't want to give up their exclusive rights to some of the best hunting in North Carolina, and the county commissioners supported them.

Governor Jim Martin stepped in and worked out a compromise – a complicated land swap. Basically all protected land on the Martin County side will be state-owned, with the exception of a 9,000-acre tract along Devils Gut, a blackwater creek especially rich in ecological diversity. This 9,000-acre tract is privately owned except for a 1,100 acre-tract that was traded by some citizens for a condominium in Florida. The North Carolina Nature Conservancy now owns this small area. The U.S. Fish and Wildlife Service and the Conservancy are negotiating to buy the remaining land to add to the Roanoke River National Wildlife Refuge.

The land that already has been acquired for the refuge is open for hunting and fishing and other public uses. The Nature Conservancy offers guided field trips to this area in the spring and fall. Adventurous paddlers and small boaters can enter the area by following the river upstream from Jamesville or by paddling Gardener Creek from Highway 64. Hunting and camping are not allowed without the permission of the current land owners.

"It's the most important single intact bottomland forest in the Mid-Atlantic region," Tommy Hughes, a state game lands biologist said of the area that will make up the refuge. "It's the best deer hunting in the state and the best wild turkey hunting Down East."

The state intends to keep it that way with strict controls. Hunters must apply for permits. A lottery in Raleigh determines who gets the permits. Those picked will be assigned to one of eight different tracts. The number of hunters in each tract is regulated and enforced. Hunters with permits may camp in designated sites, or within 100 yards of the river. Permits are not required for hunters of small game.

It's estimated that 50 to 80 deer live in each square mile of the refuge. And wild turkeys are abundant, often seen in huge flocks.

Wildlife observers are welcome at any time, but they will have to endure the same hardships as hunters to enjoy themselves. Access to this special preserve isn't easy.

At this writing, the state owns 12,959 acres in nine different tracts on the south side of the river. The land is divided into sectors, some bearing the names of former owners: Conine Island, Broadneck, Company Swamp, Speller-Outlaw, Nicholson, Urquhart, Whitley, Lindsay, Rogerson.

Conine Island near Williamston is the most accessible. It can be reached from a boat ramp in town, two parking areas off U.S. Highway 17 and by canoe from State Road 1100. Quitsna Landing near Hamilton is the boat access area for the Broadneck and Company Swamp sectors. Hiking is allowed on old logging roads that cut through the river levee forest. The Rogerson tract is accessible from State Road 1417. Speller-Outlaw, Nicholson, Urquhart, Whitley and Lindsay can only be reached by boat.

There are no designated hiking trails at this writing but unmarked hunter's paths can be found here and there. Hiking is allowed on old logging roads that cut through the river levee forest in the Broadneck and Company Swamp sectors. Hikers in other sectors will have to find their own way through the forested wetlands. Caution is advised. It's easy to become disoriented and get lost. Carry a compass and a map, and let somebody know where you intend to go and when you expect to return. Bertie County has a well trained volunteer search and rescue team, but they really don't want your business. Backpack campers are tolerated so long as they pack out all their trash.

Those willing to brave the wilds can enjoy a great diversity of wildlife in the bottomlands. Birders may spot eagles. Herons and egrets nest in seven major rookeries beside the river, the biggest concentration of these big birds in the state. This probably is the best place in the state to see wild turkeys. They roost in big flocks and can be heard gobbling all over the woods in the spring. Birders have identified 214 species along the river, including 14 varieties of waterfowl. Deer are everywhere, but bears are more numerous downstream. Owl hoots and bobcat screams may liven up the insect chorus that serenades the evening campfire.

A cable ferry runs at San Souci Crossing on the Cashie River, a tributary of the Roanoke.

Another preserve enriched by the waters of the Roanoke is Batchelor Bay Game Lands, a 9,446-acre bear sanctuary at the mouth of Albemarle Sound. This is a wet wilderness of beautiful cypress gum swamp and accessible only by boat. The water is shallow and stumpy so boaters should proceed with caution. Bald eagles nest in the area.

Canoes are especially popular on the Roanoke. Many paddlers run the river like a mountain stream, putting in upstream and taking out down. Skilled river runners looking for thrills put in at Roanoke Rapids and run through the rocks of the fall line to the last rapids at Weldon. It's a four- to six-hour run and dangerous in places. Paddlers should be experienced in class III water and go for the first time with a guide or a group that knows the water. Don't attempt this run when the water is high.

For safer and more sedate paddling, try one of the many creeks that flow into the river. Gardner's Creek on U.S. Highway 64 between

Williamston and Jamesville is a good one. It runs into the Devils Gut, which offers great sightseeing. A campground and boat ramp are by the highway at creekside.

Fishing is good all along the river and in the creeks. Stripers, large-mouth bass, catfish, bream and pickerel are often caught. If you like to fish, go to the river at least once in the spring when the herring are running and everybody catches fish. Many people clean their catches on the bank and take them to the Cypress Grill at the landing at Jamesville, where the owners will cook and serve them, a traditional feast along the Roanoke.

For more information about the Roanoke River:

Roanoke River National Wildlife Refuge
P.O. Box 430
Windsor, N.C. 27983
(919) 794-5326

Jerry Holliman and his staff are working to build visitors facilities. Meanwhile, they are happy to provide information by mail or phone. They'd love to hear from volunteers willing to build trails or help with other projects.

Bertie County Economic Development Commission
P.O. Box 588
Windsor, N.C. 27983
(919) 794-4031

Windsor is a pretty little town on the Cashie River, a tributary of the Roanoke. The town has nice parks and a zoo for children. A campground is convenient to the public boat ramp on the river and suitable for RVs. Hunting and fishing supplies and information are available at local tackle shops. Visit Hope Plantation, the home of North Carolina Governor David Stone. Ride the old fashioned San Souci cable ferry.

Martin County Economic Development Commission
305 East Main Street
P.O. Drawer 1048
Williamston, N.C. 27892
(919) 792-2044

Williamston is a pleasant river town and a good place for food, lodging and supplies. There's a public park and boat ramp near the U.S. Highway 17 bridge. Information is available at the office about re-enactments and other events at nearby Fort Branch, which is off State

Road 1416, 1.5 miles east of Hamilton. Generally, Fort Branch is open April through November on Saturdays and Sundays. Saturday hours: 10:30 a.m.-4:30 p.m. Sunday hours: 1:30 p.m.-4:30 p.m.

Port O'Plymouth
Roanoke River Museum
Historical Society of Washington County
PO Box 296
Plymouth, N.C. 27962
(919) 793-1377

Exhibits about the battle of Plymouth. Sponsors occasional living history weekends in April with Civil War demonstrations and events.

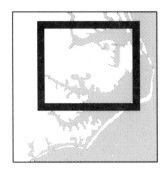

Albemarle and Pamlico Sounds

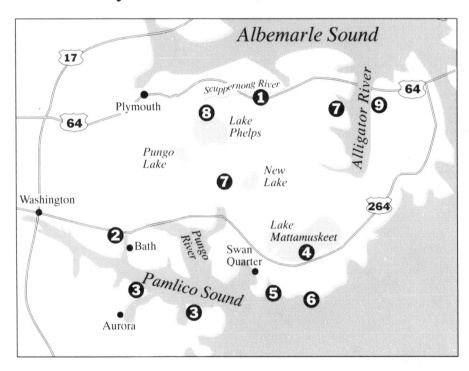

Albemarle Sound

17

64

Plymouth

64

Scuppernong River

①

⑧

Lake Phelps

⑦

Pungo Lake

New Lake

⑦

Washington

②

Bath

Pungo River

Swan Quarter

Lake Mattamuskeet

④

264

Alligator River

⑦

⑨

64

③

Pamlico Sound

⑤

⑥

③

Aurora

1. Scuppernong River
2. Goose Creek State Park
3. Goose Creek Game Lands (two sections)
4. Mattamuskeet National Wildlife Refuge
5. Swan Quarter National Wildlife Refuge
6. Gull Rock Game Lands
7. Pocosin Lakes National Wildlife Refuge (two sections)
8. Pettigrew State Park
9. Alligator River National Wildlife Refuge

The North Shore at Lake Mattamuskeet.

That sagging willow bush a canoe length away was heavy with cottonmouth. A chunky reptile lay hidden in the branches, coils expanding and contracting ominously with every breath. I couldn't see its head in the murky light of the deep swamp, but I felt that cold stare.

The little tributary of the Scuppernong River that I was exploring twisted beneath a swamp forest canopy so thick that it blocked the sun. I'd sniffed out a bream bed at the mouth of the creek earlier and used a cane pole to catch all the red-bellied perch I cared to clean and eat.

Paddling upstream in search of a rare stand of Atlantic white cedar had seemed to be an excellent way to finish this little fishing trip. But then the creek narrowed to six feet just as I encountered the moccasin's resting place. I was lucky to spot the snake in time. Had I kept going that cottonmouth could have ended up in my lap.

I floated a respectable distance away, afraid to spook the snake with a camera flash, wondering if traveling further upstream was really a good idea. In my younger days I would've just blown that snake to pieces with my trusty shotgun and felt like a dragon slaying hero. I'd been raised to believe that the only good snake was a dead snake. But my attitude toward these fellow predators has mellowed with the years.

I was on the snake's turf. But he didn't bother me, so I returned the favor and backpaddled away. I would return one wintry day when all the snakes were denned to see those big junipers.

The Scuppernong River is short – less than 20 miles long – but wildly beautiful. Its black water flows out of the swampy heart of the Albemarle-Pamlico peninsula, where more than 300 square miles of swamps and pocosins can be found. This was the last area in this part of the state to be settled by whites. Early accounts called this land the Great Eastern Dismal and considered it a "haunt for wild beasts." Vast tracts still fit that description and have been preserved in four national wildlife refuges, two state parks and several state-owned game lands. Draining, timbering and farming have tamed much of this land, but a lot of it remains wild and challenging.

Canoes once were the principal means of transportation in these parts. More than 30 ancient cypress dugouts have been found remarkably well preserved in the acidic water of Lake Phelps near Creswell. The oldest was judged to be 4,380 years old according to radio carbon tests, the second oldest canoe ever found in United States. The largest dugout ever found in the South, a 31-footer, also came from these waters.

Pottery and other artifacts leave a record of human occupation of the peninsula all the way back to the archaic Indian period from 8,000 to 1,000 years B.C. Whites were latecomers to the area. The Roanoke voyagers reported visiting Lake Mattamuskeet and the Pungo River near the current town of Belhaven in 1586.

Almost 100 years later Colonel Joshua Tarkington and Captain Thomas Miller sailed across Albemarle Sound from Edenton and explored the Scuppernong River. The first settlers didn't move to the southern shore of the sound until the early 1700's. A log fort was built near the mouth of the Alligator River for protection against pirates and hostile Indians. The area is still known as Fort Landing today and was the only white settlement on the Alligator River for many years.

The log walls didn't help much. The Indians were tired of being pushed off their land and rebelled on September 22, 1711, a terrible day in eastern Carolina. The Tuscarora from the Pamlico and Neuse Rivers allied with the Machapunga of the peninsula and attacked and killed every white person they could find. Many of the Indians had lived among whites for years before turning on their unsuspecting neighbors. Indians routinely tortured their captives. Surviving whites never forgave those atrocities and paid back in kind.

A force of South Carolina military officers and their Yamasee Indian mercenaries conquered the Tuscarora, but Machapunga guerrillas hidden in the wilderness fought on. A report from Governor Thomas Pollock tells of a raid in 1713. "The Machapungas have done us great mischief, having killed or taken about 45 on the Croatan and Alligator River. There are about 50 or 60 of them who got together between Machapungo (now Pungo) River and Roanoke Island, which is about 100 miles in length with all manner of lakes, quagmires and swamps, and is, I believe, one of the greatest deserts in the world, where it is almost impossible for white men to follow them.

"They (the Machapunga) have boats and canoes and are expert watermen so they can transport themselves wherever they please."

Peace was finally made and the Machapunga agreed to live on a reservation beside Lake Mattamuskeet. Their culture and language faded away as the Indians adopted the white man's lifestyle. Earl Pierce, the current chief of the Meherrin tribe near Ahoskie, is descended from Israel Pierce, who died in the late 1700s. Israel Pierce was the last Machapunga known to speak the native tongue.

With the Indians out of the way, the settlers devoted their time to exploiting the rich natural bounty of the land. Forests were cut to build towns, houses and ships. Vast stands of rot-resistant Atlantic white cedar used to cover the drier parts of the region. It was heavily logged along with the ancient cypress trees in the swamps. The resources seemed endless and no one thought of leaving anything for the future.

Wetlands were drained, cleared and plowed, at first with slave labor, later with tractors, draglines and bulldozers. Greedy developers and their failed schemes have left many scars across this big peninsula, but the wounds are healing as more territory is allowed to return to the wild. Some people are learning that all natural resources have to be used conservatively and that only by letting nature take its course can we have clean air and water.

Plenty of old and new wilderness waits to be explored in this land between the sounds, with the lowest human population density in the state and more bears than any other place on the East Coast.

Many areas are dangerous and difficult to maneuver in and wilderness skills and equipment are necessary for exploring them. But there are many spots as well where wildlife can be observed from the roadside, where whole families can safely stroll through the woods or swim in the river. Plenty of room here for all kinds of outdoor fun. You just need to know where to look.

Goose Creek State Park

This 1,596-acre stretch of river land between Mallard, Goose and Broad Creeks is the last wild area on the north shore of the Pamlico River. It's 10 miles east of Washington just off U.S. Highway 264. Follow the signs.

The cypress and live oak trees along the riverbank in the park serve to remind what the Pamlico River was like before development. The nearby town of Bath is the oldest incorporated city in the state and used to be a thriving and rowdy port, for a while the home of the pirate called Blackbeard. A traveling evangelist trying to bring religion to the "ungospelized wilds" arrived in Bath only to find rejection from the townspeople. In spite, he cursed the town, declaring it never would grow or prosper. The curse turned out to be a blessing. Bath remains a quiet little community off the main road, a charming place to visit.

Every mile of the Pamlico seems to have some ghost story or legend attached to it. Beside the state road leading to Goose Creek Park is the site of a fatal horse race with the devil. According to legend, a gentleman named Elliot loved to drink liquor and race horses. One Sunday morning, when he should have been on his way to church, he was drunk and en route to a horse race.

Along the way, he met a mysterious rider on a powerful horse who challenged him to a contest on the spot. Elliot took him up, shouting for everyone to hear, "I'll win this race or ride this horse to hell!"

During the race he drunkenly rode full speed into the side of a big tree, killing himself and the horse. Four deep hoofprints were evidence of the terrified animal's attempt to stop. The mysterious rider who had challenged Elliott vanished and was never seen again.

That happened in 1850 and the hoofprints are still there. Much has been written over the years about the so called Devil's Hoofprints. Curiosity seekers come to see these depressions in the ground. Many have tried to eradicate them but they always return.

In my younger and wilder days, a friend and I rode our motorcycles into the tracks, spinning our wheels and destroying them. Sure enough, the tracks were back the next morning.

Goose Creek State Park is the best place to camp and hike on the Pamlico. A dozen primitive campsites are nestled deep in the woods. I've camped here many times and had the whole place to myself.

Controlled burning has thinned the unnaturally dense undergrowth in the second growth forest around the campground. This opened a browsing area for deer and created more opportunity for wildlife watchers to study them. Hunting, of course, is not allowed in state parks, but private land around the park is heavily hunted in season. Rangers occasionally have problems with the hunters' dogs chasing deer through the park.

It's an easy walk from the campground to the river or creek. Trailer boats have to be launched across Goose Creek at Dinah's Landing, but canoes can be put in almost anywhere. Lumber used to be shipped from this landing. Big pilings still remain from the old barge dock, creating cover for fish and perches for pelicans and other birds. Anybody with a cane pole and a can of worms can catch a supper of panfish here, but those seeking bass need to go back into the creeks.

The Pamlico offers double opportunity when it comes to fishing. Both salt water and fresh water fish can be caught here, everything from catfish to giant tarpon.

Hikers at Goose Creek will find seven miles of the best trails on the Pamlico. Maps and trail conditions are available from rangers, who also offer tips about the best spots for observing wildlife. Boardwalks take hikers into the marshes and swamps. The Live Oak Trail follows the prettiest section of shoreline left on this river. The magnificent grove of ancient spreading oaks along this trail was alive when the Indians occupied this land. These trees are full of songbirds and sassy

Pelicans roost in the early morning fog at Dinah's Landing in Goose Creek State Park.

squirrels. The tracks of deer and raccoons are common along the trail. Experienced wildlife observers can see signs of many other creatures. Foxes and bobcats hunt here at night. Bears pass through occasionally. Other wildlife is more easily visible. Otters, minks, muskrats and marsh rabbits swim through the creeks and disappear in the marsh grass. Ospreys perch in the dead trees beside the river and quiet viewers can watch them pluck fish from the water and carry their catch back to the nest. Red cockaded woodpeckers have staked out part of the pinewoods as they work their way back from near extinction. Wood ducks can be seen year round and various diving ducks return to the river in the winter.

Hikers here can cool off at a lovely river beach, where the water is shallow and without dangerous currents. Adults can wade hundreds of yards from shore and still be only waist-deep. Kids love this beach.

Halfway between the beach and the parking lot is a shady picnic ground with a nice view of the river, a perfect spot for a family outing.

Goose Creek Game Land

Pamlico Point is a marshy peninsula at the mouth of the Pamlico River. Once a military bombing range, it's now the premier spot for waterfowl hunting in North Carolina, according to Tommy Hughes, an avid duck hunter who also happens to be a state biologist in charge of all the eastern game lands.

The point is part of the Goose Creek Game Land, which has 7,599 acres of intensely managed waterfowl impoundments, natural marshes, pocosin pine woods and a large tract of old-growth cypress in the Gum Swamp section. Unlike the state park of the same name, this land is managed for hunting.

Dirt roads run through some of the drier wooded parts of the game lands and can be reached from State Highways 33 and 304. They're passable most of the time but a good rain can turn them into quagmires. Metal gates usually are locked except during hunting season.

Hikers are welcome to use the roads so long as they don't block the gates with their vehicles. It's best to come on non-hunting days. Hiking here during deer hunting season can be dangerous and anybody who does it should at least wear a blaze orange hat or vest. No hunting is allowed on Sunday and that's a good time to come to hike. Primitive camping is allowed near Hoboken Fire Tower. There is no charge and no permits are needed, but campers are expected to keep the area clean and put out campfires.

A boat is needed to get to many of the marshy areas. Wildlife officials recommend a 16-footer with lots of freeboard and at least a 25-horsepower outboard for any trip to Pamlico Point. They cringe at the thought of canoes or kayaks in these waters. Only experienced open-water paddlers in good sea kayaks should attempt this trip.

A cryptic note on the official game lands map assures readers that Pamlico Point is considered 90 percent free of explosives left over from the days when the area was a bombing range. No one I talked to ever had heard of anyone getting blown up and hunters use the area regularly.

But the water stays rough here, and it gets very dangerous in bad weather. Boats can be launched from Oyster Creek Landing at the end of State Road 1235. Duck hunters leave before dawn when the water is calm and use bright spotlights to keep from running over the numerous fishing nets and crab pots. A stiff sea breeze and swells usually develop as the sun climbs toward mid-morning and warms the air and water. Rain gear and warm clothing are suggested.

Some hunters tow smaller boats to use in the four shallow 200-acre impoundments at the point that were created as mosquito-control ponds. No gasoline engines are allowed in the ponds.

Small skiffs or canoes can handle the trip to the Campbell's Creek and Spring Creek impoundments located on the west bank of Goose Creek just east of Highway 33. Alligators have been spotted here so it's not advisable to let dogs swim in these waters.

Most duck hunters at the point wear waders. The average depth of the impoundments is about 18 inches, but there are occasional holes. Eight permanent duck blinds are available on a first-come, first-served basis. Birders are welcome to use the blinds out of hunting season. Most hunters just conceal themselves in the marsh with camouflage netting.

Mostly puddle duck species come to Pamlico Point but when big northeast winds start blowing a lot of diving ducks take cover in the marshes. Geese and swans may turn up. The best hunting is at the beginning of the season. The ducks get gun shy later on and decoy spreads and skilled calling are required to bring them in.

Water levels in these man-made ponds is controlled with a system of pipes and pumps, and crabs love these ponds. Crabbers near the water-control structures can fill a cooler in no time when the pumps are running.

Duck hunters have to apply for a limited number of permits that are chosen in Raleigh by computer. Usually 60 hunters are allowed each day for three days out of the week at Pamlico Point, 24 more at Campbell's Creek. Usually, there's a three-day season in October for the abundant teal. The season opens again in November. Each hunter can take three ducks per day, and the bag can include one pintail, black duck, hen mallard or hooded merganser and two redheads. Special permits are required for swan. Hunting is closed for now on canvasbacks and Canada geese, but hunters report seeing more canvasbacks every year. Mild winters have been keeping geese in Delaware, Maryland and Virginia. Seasons are reviewed from year to year and subject to change. Hunters should stay current to avoid fines.

Hunting for deer and small game is allowed in these lands, and the deer hunting is especially good. Biologists plant clover along the shore of Goose Creek to attract them. Quail hunting is getting better all the time. As in most game lands, small game such as rabbits and squirrels is underhunted.

Some very big bears are seen on the gameland, and a study is under way to find out why. One hunter killed a 727-pound bear on private

Wild geese fly over Pamlico Point.

Biologist/angler Fred Bonner with a brace of bass. He says the Pamlico River is excellent for fishing.

land just a few miles away during the 1990 season, a state record. Bears are getting to be a minor nuisance in the area, often coming into towns looking for food and scaring people. Farmers complain that they destroy crops and steal pigs. An Aurora homeowner had to evict a sow and two cubs from the crawl space of his house on a residential street a couple of years ago. Caution is advised when hiking or hunting at Goose Creek. Never feed bears and never get between a sow and her cubs.

Wildlife observers can spot bald eagles around the impoundments at Pamlico Point. Egrets, white ibis and herons live in the marshes. Colonies of endangered red-cockaded woodpeckers are doing well in the pine woods.

Summer brings the usual hosts of insects and snakes. Four species of poisonous vipers are known to live here. Local folks shoot all snakes on sight and tell of cottonmouths with heads the size of a man's fist. But no snakebites have been reported around here.

Fishing can be outstanding for flounder, speckled trout and puppy drum. Biologists report that plenty of trophy tarpon migrate between here and Florida but not many people fish for them. Striped bass are making a comeback thanks to restrictive limits set by the state. Large-mouth bass anglers do well in the upper reaches of the creeks that flow through the game lands.

A large French-owned open-pit phosphate mine operates near the mouth of the river. It's the biggest industry in Beaufort County and has a lot of political clout. It also has been the source of much pollution in the Pamlico River. But pressure from the state and conservation groups has caused the company to upgrade equipment and reduce discharges into the river.

A local conservation group, the Pamlico-Tar River Foundation, monitors the river and is trying to clean it up. Industrial, agricultural and municipal polluters are beginning to respond to pressure the save the river and the wildlife it sustains.

Fred Bonner is an International Game Fish Association biologist from Aurora who fishes a lot and knows the waters of eastern Carolina.

"The Pamlico River has some outstanding fishing, but those environmentalists are trying to scare everybody off the river by saying it's polluted," he says. "If they spent more time on the river and less time raising money they'd know it's just not as bad as they say it is."

Surely, the river is beginning to recover, thanks to the efforts of people who know and love it. And it still offers plenty of natural beauty for those who seek it.

Mattamuskeet National Wildlife Refuge

Mattamuskeet is the largest natural lake in North Carolina but no one is sure how it got there. An English expedition found it in 1585, but Indians had lived on its shoreline for several thousand years. According to Indian legend this lake – 16 miles long by six miles wide, with an average depth of three feet – was formed after a great fire burned a shallow depression in the flammable peat and was flooded by heavy rains. No natural streams or springs feed the lake, only rain.

Modern scientists theorize that Mattamuskeet and other Carolina Bay lakes are craters from a prehistoric meteor shower or were created by wind and wave action from the last ice age. Whatever the lake's origin, game and fish were abundant and the lakeshore provided a happy hunting ground to the small tribe that called themselves Machapunga, or People of the Trembling Earth – referring to the spongy peat found in the area. In some places, a person can jump up and down on the ground and shake someone standing 100 feet away.

Mattamuskeet means "a moving swamp" in the Algonquin tongue, but the swamp didn't move fast enough for the white man. Attempts to drain the 75-square-mile lake and farm the 50,000 acres of fertile bottomland – considered the best in the world – began as early as 1773. It took 20th century engineering to finally pump out the lake and put it to the plow.

In 1913 the world's largest pumping station was built to drain the lake. It had four steam engines that could move 1,000,000 gallons of water a minute, and it soon pumped the lake dry. Farms, a town, a railroad, even a prison occupied the lake bed at various times. But the water returned. Three times the lake was drained, and three times it stubbornly refilled, until the Great Depression and heavy rains washed out the project for good. Farming the lake bed just wasn't profitable enough to keep the pumps running.

With the return of the water came wild geese, ducks and swans, happy to regain their ancient winter home. The lake and its surrounding swampwoods and marshes was sold to the U.S. Fish and Wildlife Service, and the Mattamuskeet National Wildlife Refuge was established in 1934. The money for the lake came from hunting license fees and taxes on sporting arms and equipment. Civilian Conservation Corps workers – those heroes of the Great Depression – converted the three-story concrete and steel pumping station into a 15,000-square-foot hunting lodge and hotel.

Edward Cuthrell of Swan Quarter remembers when Mattamuskeet

was farmland. "I helped plant the last crop in the lake," he recalled. "Got paid 12 and half cents per hour."

Cuthrell later joined the Civilian Conservation Corps and helped turn the pumping station into a lodge. After the lodge opened, he guided hunters on the lake. "I really enjoyed hunting and enjoyed people," he said. "I got to meet people from all walks of life." Guides were paid well to get clients to the blinds in flat bottom boats, set out decoys, then call the ducks and geese into shotgun range.

Hunters flocked to Mattamuskeet for the best goose hunting in the world. Mattamuskeet Lodge became the center of social and economic activity for the residents of Hyde County, hosting everything from high school proms to political rallies. But in the early '70s, the numbers of wild geese began to decline because of warmer winters.

"When we get winters in October like we did in the 1950s, we'll see Mattamuskeet as the goose capitol of the world again," said Edwin "Booger" Harris, another local hunting guide. "Or maybe our children will see it."

Fewer geese meant fewer hunters and Mattamuskeet Lodge went out of business. The lodge stood abandoned until July 20, 1990, when 145 people from all over North Carolina and Virginia – the Friends of Mattamuskeet Lodge – joined with National Wildlife Refuge workers in the sweltering heat to begin the second restoration of this National Historic building. Hard working volunteers – including Edward Cuthrell and other former members of the Civilian Conservation Corps – began cleaning and making repairs.

Royden Clark, a banker from nearby Engelhard was chosen to lead the restoration project. "We have a challenge to meet," he said. "Our goal is total restoration of the lodge."

Inspections by engineers found much wrong with the old lodge. Extensive structural work must be done. Refuge manager Don Temple estimates the restoration could cost as much as four million dollars.

"We will continue to make repairs and stabilize the structure so it doesn't deteriorate any further," he said. A contract has been awarded for roof repairs, but this is just a holding action. Money isn't available for more extensive work, but fund raising continues and more volunteers are getting involved.

The North Carolina General Assembly awarded $50,000 to the East Carolina University Regional Development Institute for a feasibility study on restoring the lodge and the potential economic benefits.

"The lodge used to be a center of commercial activity," said Janice Faulkner, the institute's director. "That economic base has been lost.

The Mattamuskeet Lodge, with its 125-foot smokestack as an observation tower, is a major landmark in Hyde County. But the building remains closed until money is raised for its restoration. Don Temple, manager of the Lake Mattamuskeet National Wildlife Refuge, estimates restoration could cost as much as four million dollars.

Ospreys are returning from the brink of extinction, and can be found nesting in the trees at Lake Mattamuskeet.

We're trying to help the local people out by putting the lodge back to productive use, like it used to be."

The institute asked the citizens of Hyde County for opinions through a hearing and survey, then proposed a plan. The building would serve as a museum and research station to study and display the rich ecological diversity of Hyde County.

The building would provide plenty of space for offices and rooms for meetings and seminars. Special events could be held in the lodge, just as in the old days.

The Lake Mattamuskeet National Wildlife Refuge already attracts about 60,000 visitors annually. Many more might come, or stop while passing through on their way to the Outer Banks, if something attracted them. Nature and the museum might do that. Plans call for local guides to offer visitors scenic boat rides around the lake. A network of footpaths and canoe trails would provide a close look at the treasures of Mattamuskeet. Bed and breakfast inns might spring up for guests looking for a place to get away from it all for a few days.

The lodge – with its 125-foot smokestack as an observation tower – is a major landmark in Hyde County. But the building remains closed until money is raised for its restoration. Still, visitors can picnic on the grounds, fish in the canals or hike the trails.

The whole refuge is a wildlife watcher's delight. Alligators make themselves at home in certain canals. Bears prowl the dense woods and swamps. Deer feed beside the roads and trails. Birders have identified more than 200 species around the lake. Ospreys and bald eagles patrol the shallow water. Otters and nutria play in the numerous drainage canals. A causeway on N.C. Highway 94 divides the lake and provides easy access for fishers and wildlife watchers.

Thousands of arctic tundra swans – about one fifth of the world's population – return to the lake each winter to fill the skies with great white wings and haunting calls. It's always a thrill when the swans return. This annual migration has been featured in a National Geographic television program. Here you can actually see it, and staff members at the refuge provide guided tours to see the swans in December.

Some waterfowl hunting is allowed on the lake but it's carefully controlled. However, several guides in the area offer hunts on private land nearby for waterfowl, quail, deer, bear and pheasant. The lake is surrounded by some of the most productive farm land in the world and wildlife feasts on these fields. Hunting and fishing at Mattamuskeet is exceptional and attracts people from all over the country.

The lake is known as one of the best bass fishing spots anywhere, but it must be waded or fished with a shallow-draft boat. Modern bass boats can't function here. All boats are banned between November and March but fishermen can use the causeway all year. The local volunteer fire department holds an annual bass tournament to raise money and the catches have been outstanding. All tournament fish are examined by biologists then released alive into the lake. Anglers have to share the resource with the abundant ospreys that nest in the cypress trees in the middle of the lake. Many of the bass caught here have talon scars on their backs from narrow escapes.

Bass used to be caught mainly around the bases of the cypress trees but now they're more apt to be hooked in the open water and grass beds. Trolling with a spoon is very effective.

Big catfish and stripers also are caught in the lake. White perch are caught on cane poles near the causeway bridges. Herring dippers work the Outfall Canal leading from the lodge. I've caught the biggest crabs I've ever seen from this lake.

Motels, restaurants and tackle shops can be found near the lake. Primitive camping is available at Leslie's Landing on the north shore, just west of the causeway. Lakeside campsites are shaded by big cypress trees next to the boat ramp.

Wetlands such as those at Mattamuskeet used to be considered worthless until drained. Now it's understood that our swamps and marshes control floods, clean up pollution and provide habitat for wildlife and seafood. One hunting guide here estimates that intact wetlands are worth at far more as they are than for any other use to which they could be put. Mattamuskeet proves it.

Swan Quarter National Wildlife Refuge

The Swan Quarter National Wildlife Refuge is a 15,500-acre expanse of marshy islands and peninsulas on the edge of the Pamlico Sound not far from Lake Mattamuskeet. Most of the land is pocosin and pine woods, but one notable 85-acre tract of old-growth cypress survives on Juniper Bay.

There's a local tale about a murderous bootlegger who hid out in this marshy wilderness right after World War II. The law never found him and he stayed here until he died. The ruins of his cabin have been reclaimed by the swamp. A fugitive who knew how to survive in a swamp probably could hide out in here today. It's that wild and remote.

A fishing pier at Bell Island off Highway 264 that extends 1,100 feet into Rose Bay is the only public access to the refuge. Anglers make good catches of spots, croakers, sea trout and white perch from the pier at times, but the fishing often is poor. The pier is open from sunrise until refuge officials arrive to close it around dusk.

A boat is the only way to really see this refuge. The marshes and creeks can be explored with ease in a canoe. The open water bays that border on the Pamlico Sound are windy and subject to rough conditions. Have enough boat for the job, and if you venture into the sound keep a close eye on the weather. Hardly a year goes by without some fisherman losing his life out here.

Speckled trout fishing is outstanding in these creeks and bays starting in late June. Anglers run Mirro lures at different depths until they hit them. Fresh shrimp will do the job for trout, flounder and the occasional puppy drum.

This is a reptile's paradise with a growing alligator population and 29 species of snakes. Of special concern is the diminutive Carolina Pygmy Rattler, locally called water rattler, ground rattler or red rattler. This snake is becoming rare but there's a good population here along with the larger canebrake rattlers, cottonmouths and copperheads. Amateur herpetologists (they don't like being called snake hunters) have a ball here.

Once when I was launching a canoe from a private landing in Rose Bay, a snake crawled out from under my truck as I was taking the canoe off. A second snake left the bank where I was putting in the canoe. and still another swam across the canal as I paddled toward the marsh. Three snake sightings in less than five minutes. Gave me something to think about when I made camp that night.

Ospreys, eagles and hawks soar over this refuge in large numbers. Wading birds work the marshes, and logs in the water are covered with turtles. Plenty of deer and bear live here but the vegetation is so dense they're hard to see. Some people claim to have seen cougars here, but like all such sightings, they're unconfirmed.

Winter is the time to come to this refuge. There are no mosquitos and snakes to cause misery and fear then, but there are thousands of ducks in the bays, buffleheads, canvasbacks, redheads and others. Swans and geese also winter here. Waterfowl hunting is allowed within a well marked 6,120-acre hunting area on Great Island, Marsh Island and part of the mainland on Juniper Bay. All federal regulations apply. The rest of the refuge is closed to waterfowl hunting but determined birders may look and photograph all they want.

Gull Rock Game Lands

The state owns 19,436 acres of hardwood flats, pocosin, swamp forest and brackish marshes on the Pamlico Sound between West Bluff Bay and Benson's Point.

Turn off U.S. Highway 264 at the New Holland intersection and follow State Road 1164 beside the Outfall Canal for about six miles.

There's a boat ramp at the end of the road, but it's in poor condition. Small skiffs and canoes can be launched with difficulty. Crabbing and herring dipping in the canal can be excellent. Speckled trout, puppy drum and flounder can be caught in the open waters of the sound.

Hikers will find trails beside the canals that can be reached from dirt roads. The best hiking is in the Hydeland area where an abandoned railroad bed leads through an old-growth sweet gum forest. Other trails lead to a forested island surrounded by marsh. Several beautiful, isolated stands of bald cypress rise out of the extensive marshes in this preserve and some of them can be reached on foot, although I would advise waterproof boots, especially after heavy rains. Access is improving every year.

This is a bear sanctuary. Wildlife watchers need to go in July when the blackberries and wild cherries are ripening and the bears are in rut. Bears often are seen then walking the roads or feeding in the plots of clover and milo that are planted to attract game.

Deer hunting and duck hunting are the most popular activities here, but biologist Tommy Hughes reports that hunting pressure is minimal. Waterfowl concentrates in the well-managed impoundments and the soundside marshes. For some reason, most of the birds tend to arrive after hunting season. Pintail, mallards, widgeon and blue wing teal are most often seen in the marshes, especially when they're flooded by wind-driven high tides.

Diving ducks inhabit the open water of the sound. Swans and geese are apt to show up. Prime waterfowl viewing times here are from February until mid-March.

A few alligators abide here, along with the usual snakes and turtles. Otters and raccoons are especially abundant. Ospreys nest around the waterfowl impoundments and eagles use this area as well.

Gull Rock Game Lands is a more accessible refuge than the one at Swan Quarter but it's just as wild. Camping is allowed in designated areas.

Pocosin Lakes National Wildlife Refuge

This is the newest refuge on the Albemarle-Pamlico peninsula. But this land almost ended up as a Japanese open-pit peat mine. At the last minute the Conservation Fund and the Richard King Mellon Foundation purchased more than 93,000 acres of the land – the old First Colony Farms property – and donated it the U.S. Fish and Wildlife Service on June 26, 1990. The existing Pungo National Wildlife Refuge and the 6,000-acre section of Alligator River National Wildlife Refuge around Frying Pan Lake were incorporated into the new refuge. The eight million dollar purchase was the largest donation ever made to the federal government.

First Colony Farms was a corporate farming operation owned by German and Japanese investors. The company stripped thousands of acres of forest bare and drained the wetlands. Bulldozers and giant tractors plowed fields that stretched to the horizon.

The trees cut to create the fields were not harvested, just bulldozed into rows and burned. The glow from these fires could be seen for miles at night. When the wind was right, the smoke could be smelled all the way to Greenville – almost a hundred miles away. Once beautiful wilderness began to look like the outskirts of hell.

Deer that ate the farm's crops were shot and hauled out by the truckload, or left to rot in the fields. Agricultural pesticide and herbicide runoff flowed down the canals into the sounds and damaged the traditional commercial and sport fishing industry. State and local governments enjoyed the increased tax base and allowed the land to be raped, ignoring warnings from their own environmental experts.

First Colony Farms was promoted as the economic salvation of eastern Carolina but it went bankrupt, proving that environmentally unsound practices are bad business. Japanese investors moved in to buy the land to mine the peat that lies under the soil and burn it in a power plant which would have been located in the same area. But they did not buy it. They were outbid for the land by the Environmental Defense Fund. This open pit mine with its resulting air and water pollution would have been an environmental disaster even worse than that caused by First Colony Farms.

But a big fire swept through the peat bogs on this land in 1985, burning more than 20,000 acres. In places the fire burned three feet into the ground.

This savaged land remains vulnerable to fire, and refuge officials are trying to figure out how the 90 miles of poorly maintained canals

Red fox cubs rest and
play in the Pocosin
Lakes National
Wildlife Refuge.

left by the farming operation were supposed to work so they can keep the peat partially flooded and prevent future fires. That will allow the land to recover.

Most of this refuge is still green, however, dense with shrubs and scrubby pines. A lot of the fields are growing back in sedge and offer some of the best quail hunting in the state. More than 2,000 acres are covered with hardwoods and loblolly pines. Atlantic white cedar can be found on eight different tracts around the Scuppernong River. Presently, the U.S. Fish and Wildlife Service operates the refuge.

The refuge includes most of the 4,100-acre New Lake (also known as Alligator Lake), the 2,800-acre Pungo Lake, and Frying Pan Lake, which covers more than 2,000 acres. Four and a half miles of shoreline on Lake Phelps also have been taken into the refuge.

County commissioners have traditionally opposed the establishment of wildlife refuges because it removes land from the tax roles. This refuge might never have been established if not for a new policy by the federal government which allows a fee to be paid to local governments equal to the tax revenue the land would have generated if privately owned. The Wildlife Service plans to further aid the area economy by providing recreational facilities in the refuge.

Foremost in these plans is a waterfront visitors center on the Scuppernong River in Columbia on U.S. Highway 64. It is estimated that 1.3 million tourists pass Columbia each year on their way to the Outer Banks. Local officials are optimistic that the new center will cause many of them to stop and that restaurants, motels, campgrounds and other businesses will spring up to serve them. The Pocosin Lakes project, as it is being called, is being closely watched as a model of cooperation between national wildlife refuges and local citizens.

The visitors center will serve as an educational center about this wilderness area. A network of interpretive trails will lead from the center through the nearby bottomlands and pocosins to allow visitors to experience nature first hand. The Nature Conservancy also owns land along the Scuppernong and plans formal hiking and canoe trails along this pristine blackwater river.

"We're still working on our public use plan," said refuge manage Jim Savery. "The local government and citizens have been very receptive. The proposed visitors center would be a gold mine for them."

Fishing is one attraction that will bring people to this area. It is best in the Scuppernong River, Lake Phelps and Frying Pan Lake. New Lake has some bull heads and black crappie. A few channel catfish and bullheads are caught in Pungo Lake. Both of these lakes have naturally acidic water, however, that keeps fish populations low. Wintering waterfowl like these lakes just fine, though.

The entire refuge is a bear sanctuary and the north side of Pungo Lake is the best place to catch a glimpse of one. Hunters most often see them along the edges of fields here early in the morning, and dozens have been counted.

Plenty of deer roam here and the bigger ones are found near Pungo Lake where they fatten on the grain planted for waterfowl. Hunters need to apply in advance for permits to hunt the Pungo Unit. Only 250 permits are issued after a public drawing in August. Deer hunting is allowed with bows, blackpowder rifles and shotguns. It's against the rules to run deer with dogs. Special seasons and limits apply in the Pungo Unit and are subject to review and change every year.

Bird hunters may use pointers and retrievers to hunt the abundant quail, woodcocks, doves, and snipe in the refuge. All modern rifles are prohibited with the exception of .22s for squirrel hunting.

Camping, open fires, permanent blinds and baiting are not allowed. All hunters must be properly licensed and wear the required blaze orange. Vehicles must remain on designated roads and all firearms aboard must be unloaded. Night hunts are allowed by special permit for raccoons and opossums but firelighting is forbidden. State and federal officers patrol the refuge and enforce all regulations. A free map and copy of the hunting regulations is available from refuge headquarters located on State Road 1183 on the west bank of Lake Phelps.

Pettigrew State Park

Lake Phelps is the second largest natural lake in North Carolina, but it wasn't even discovered by white settlers until 1755 when a couple of hunters stumbled onto it. Archeological evidence suggests that even the Indians only came here seasonally to hunt and fish.

The lake once was called Scuppernong, Algonquin for place of the sweet bay tree. It later was renamed for Josiah Phelps, the hunter who ran through the woods to be first to touch the water after his partner sighted the lake from a tree top.

The origin of this lake, like that of Lake Mattamuskeet, is shrouded in mystery, but the current theory is that wind and wave action from the last ice age scoured out this shallow depression in the peat. And like Lake Mattamuskeet, many attempts have been made to drain it so the land beneath it could be farmed.

Slaves dug a six-mile canal from the lake to the Scuppernong River in 1786 in one such attempt. That canal remains. It runs right beside Somerset Place, a plantation house built of heart cypress in 1830. The house has been restored as a historic site and is open to visitors. Descendants of the slaves who worked the plantation gather for annual reunions to honor their ancestors.

The Pettigrew Plantation adjoined Somerset Place. It was the home of General James Johnson Pettigrew, a Confederate general who died at the Battle of Gettysburg. Both plantations fell on hard times after the Civil War and never regained their former glory. The government finally took over the land during the depression years of the 1930s and Pettigrew State Park was established – named for the general who lies buried on park property.

"There's some unique natural areas here," said Sid Shearin, the park's superintendent. "Lake Phelps and White Lake are the only clear lakes in North Carolina. Nothing drains into them, everything drains away from them, which makes them among the cleanest, most pristine lakes in the United States. But Lake Phelps has a rich wildlife population here that you won't find at White Lake, because there the shoreline is heavily developed with houses and businesses."

There are other mysteries about Lake Phelps. Its water is very acidic and supposedly largemouth bass can't reproduce in it, but they do and no one really knows how. A rare minnow, the Waccamaw Killifish, is found only here and at Lake Waccamaw in the southeastern section of the state.

The acidic water acts as a preservative, which is why so many ancient Indian canoes have been found here. Archeologists don't just find pottery shards here, they find whole pots, which is rare indeed. Visitors can view some of these artifacts at the interpretive center next to the boat ramp.

Superintendent Shearing is an admitted "tree nut" and loves to talk about the state champion trees found in the park. They include devil's walkingstick, pawpaw, sugarberry, sweetleaf and swamp tupelo. Shearing leads an annual "Big Tree" walk every November.

A mature cypress swamp forest shades the north shore of the lake and can easily be seen by hikers on the historic Carriage Trail, where the plantation owners once took horse and buggy rides along the shore.

The trail starts at the park office, passes the adjacent Somerset Place Historic Site and runs about a mile through the forest to a wildlife viewing platform at Bee Tree Canal Overlook, a great place to view waterfowl in the winter. In recent years, Lake Phelps has been one of the best places to see large flocks of Canada geese.

A short side trail leads to General Pettigrew's grave. Plans call for blazing a new trail beyond the Bee Tree Canal with assistance from Carolina Power & Light Co. and environmental groups. The new trail will be 10 miles long, making it the longest state park trail in North Carolina, according to the superintendent.

The trail now follows the lakeshore west for three miles and ends at the Moccasin Overlook, a 350-foot boardwalk through a mature cypress swamp forest. This is a great spot to fish or observe wildlife. The diversity of plant life along the shore creates an appealing habitat for lots of wildlife.

Owls and ospreys makes their homes in the majestic trees. Herons and egrets stalk the shallow waters of the lake. Minks and muskrats swim in the cypress swamp. Foxes and bobcats prowl here as well, though seldom seen. Copperheads and canebrake rattlers are common but cottonmouths are rare in the park. Most of the water snakes seen are northern and brown water snakes.

The park's campground has 13 sites, some in the shade and others in a grassy meadow. Grills, picnic tables and a central bathhouse are furnished. There are no RV hookups. A primitive campground is located off the Carriage Trail near the Bee Tree canal for scout groups and the like but reservations are required.

One of the prettiest picnic grounds anywhere is beside the road leading to the boat ramp in a large cypress grove. The lake is popular with bass fishermen and the ramp area is often crowded. Lake Phelps is very shallow and like all such bodies of water, it can get dangerous in a hurry when the wind picks up or a storm blows through. Boaters should always be alert. There's an old saying Down East: If you don't like the weather, just wait a few minutes and it will change.

Each September the park honors Native Americans with a week of special activities. School groups come to sample Indian cuisine, learn how to tan animal skins, throw a spear with a distance enhancing device called an atlatl and see the many exhibits. Special tours and field trips can be arranged with advance notice.

The park owns land on the remote south shore of the lake and rangers are trying to construct a fishing pier and picnic area there with volunteer labor and donated materials.

This is the biggest state park in North Carolina, and it has much to offer the wilderness lover. It is easily accessible, just off U.S. Highway 64 near Roper. Signs direct the way.

The Alligator River National
Wildlife Refuge is managed as
a wildlife habitat for threatened and endangered species,
including the red wolf.

Alligator River National Wildlife Refuge

The howl of the wolf can again be heard in eastern Carolina, thanks
to the Alligator River National Wildlife Refuge.

It took the North Carolina Nature Conservancy more than five
years, but in 1984, it persuaded Prudential Insurance Co. to donate this
200-square-mile expanse of log woods and swamps in Dare, Hyde and
Tyrell counties to the U.S. Fish and Wildlife Service. It's now managed
as wildlife habitat for threatened and endangered species, including the
red wolf.

U.S. Highways 64 and 264 roughly divide this refuge into thirds.
The broad Alligator River bounds the west side, Albemarle Sound the
north. The Croatan and Pamlico Sounds create the eastern boundary.
Some 45,000 acres of Air Force and Navy bombing ranges join the
southern edge of the preserve.

Red wolves used to be native to this area and most of the South.
Smaller than their timber wolf cousins, the red wolves inhabited
swamps and hunted at night. Perceived as threats to livestock, they

were almost wiped out by hunting, trapping and poisoning and were declared extinct in the wild in 1980.

But some remained in captivity, and in 1986 several were released into this refuge, marking the first attempt to restore an extinct species to the wild. This experiment is being closely watched worldwide. It may serve as the blueprint for biologists to re-introduce Sumatran tigers and Javanese rhinos back into the wild.

Captive wolves are kept penned on the refuge in the remote Sandy Ridge area, which is closed to the public. Great care is taken to keep the wolves isolated from humans. After a period of acclimation and medical exams the wolves are fitted with radio-tracking collars and released. About 30 wolves now live free on the refuge. Several have died due to various causes: road kills, drownings and fights with other wolves. The wolves have reproduced in the wild, however, and a third generation of wild-born cubs now has a chance to survive.

"This is no zoo," said Mike Phillips, the biologist in charge of the project. "Once released wolves have to make their own living. The Indians have a saying, 'A wolf is fed by its feet.' Wolves have been known to cover 50 square miles a night while hunting. Raccoons, rabbits, frogs and turtles are the usual prey for our wolves. Sometimes they'll work together to bring down a deer, sort of like a Sunday dinner."

Phillips is interested in sightings of these wolves, and anyone spotting one should call the refuge office at (919) 473-1131 and report it.

"I look forward to a time when I won't know how many wolves are out there," Phillips said.

Hunters are allowed in this refuge in areas marked on the maps available from the refuge headquarters in Manteo. Maps also are posted on 16 hunter information boards scattered across the refuge.

Access is by 150 miles of old logging roads. After hard rains these roads can mire the best four-wheel-drives and winches are advised.

Two hunters got stuck on one of these roads during the 1992 season. As they tried to push their vehicle out of the mud one of them was struck on the hand by a copperhead. His buddy made him comfortable then ran several miles to the nearest highway for help. The snake-bitten hunter was finally rescued and taken to the nearest hospital more than 50 miles away in Elizabeth City.

Hunting is during daylight hours with access allowed one hour before and after legal shooting hours. Blinds and stands must be removed at day's end. Firearms must be unloaded while transported in a vehicle or boat under power. Dog hunting is permitted only in designated areas. Young hunters must be accompanied by adults. Camping is not allowed.

Officers of the N.C. Wildlife Resources Commission and the U.S. Fish and Wildlife Service enforce these rules. Regulations are listed on the free maps but be sure to check with the refuge headquarters for any changes or updates before hunting.

Deer are the most sought game in this 145,000-acre preserve. They tend to be small, especially in the pocosins, the evergreen shrub bogs that are nutrient poor. But plenty of deer roam here, and bucks with 12- to 14-point racks have been taken.

Jimmy Berry, a commercial fisherman and trapper from Manteo, has hunted the area all of his life – carrying on a long family tradition. He estimates that 150 or more Alligator River deer have fallen to his rifle, shotgun and bow over the last 32 years. He's taken several eight-pointers and one nine-pointer from the refuge and reports that a friend of his, Bruce Creef, took a 14-pointer with a 16-inch spread while dog hunting near the bombing range – the biggest deer he's ever heard about being killed in the refuge. Average deer here dress out at 100 pounds, a nice buck 125.

Berry mostly hunts with a bow these days and has taken home the annual trophy by the Dare County Archers several times.

"The best way to kill a deer in there is to stand hunt on the ground or up a tree," he reports. "The deer feed on the old roadbeds that are covered with grass. You can stand on the roadside and stalk them with the wind in your face. I've killed a many a deer like that. The best way is to find a tree on the shoulder of the road and get up high, then wait for the deer to come down the road to you. I'd say 90 percent of the hunters just ride around in their vehicles until they spot a deer and then get out and stalk it."

The woods and vegetation bordering the roads is about as dense as anything you'll ever see – often described as impenetrable – but not to hunters like Jimmy Berry.

"I don't like to hunt the roads where the public is allowed to drive. If I do hunt those areas, I'll get way back in the woods," he said. "I like to get as far back as possible on the cable roads with a bicycle. The deer are calm, not spooked. There are no vehicles running them off the roads.

"I use a thirty-thirty for rifle hunting but I really like my shotgun. I've killed more deer with buckshot. The woods are kind of thick. It never fails, you'll find the biggest deer in the worst, over-grown terrain possible, about two miles from any road."

Some of Berry's fondest memories are of dog hunting with his father. "You go out early morning and turn the dogs loose. When they strike a deer you trail them until they jump it. Sometimes the deer will run 30 to 40 minutes then give up, then sometimes they'll run all day and you'll never see the deer. Many times the deer will go to water and it's all over for that day. It can be a job rounding all your dogs up."

Some dog hunters use radio-tracking collars to keep up with their hounds. These collars are similar to the ones on the red wolves that roam the refuge. Biologists have gotten very adept at tracking the wolves in spite of the additional signals from the dogs.

Striper fishing particularly is excellent in the Alligator River, but boaters should be experienced before taking on this river, which is two to three miles wide in places. It's more like a sound than a river and it can get rough quickly when the wind picks up, especially a northeaster. Small craft advisories are common. For a really scenic boat ride, explore the many creeks that wander off the main river and lead to natural swampy lakes deep in the wild. Alligators live in these creeks and flocks of waterfowl seek them out each winter.

Canoes and other small boats can be put in at Milltail Creek on the end of the Old Buffalo City Road that runs from U.S. 64. Paddlers have to go under an old wooden canal bridge to get in the creek. Tap it with a paddle first to chase off any snakes that may be lurking there.

This creek offers the easiest access to the interior. At the old Buffalo City site the creek widens into cypress-lined Boat Bay Lake. On the north end of the lake is a narrow, snake-and-alligator-infested stream called Sandy Ridge Gut, which leads to Sawyer Lake. I heard wolves howling on my last trip there. Sent a shiver right down my spine.

Buffalo City was a logging boom town here at the turn of the century. It had its own bank and currency. Atlantic white cedar – known around here as juniper – was cut and shipped on the company railroad. This rot-resistant wood is prized for boat building. A cholera epidemic killed most of the residents of Buffalo City. Some old pilings around the shore of Boat Bay Lake are all that's left of the once busy waterfront at Buffalo City.

This refuge contains some of the finest swamp forest left in the world – wild, spooky, hauntingly beautiful and so remote that it offered refuge for illegal activities. This area became famous for its bootleg liquor during Prohibition. East Lake Rye, as it was called, was shipped up and down the East Coast in speedboats powered by airplane engines. One of the more notorious rum-runners reformed and went on to become a well respected sheriff of Dare County.

East Lake, where much of the moonshining was centered, is north of U.S. 64. It's now an excellent place to catch largemouth bass and stripers. A state boat ramp provides access. Hunting with dogs is permitted around East Lake, but few roads traverse this wilderness.

Just south of U.S. 64, crops are raised for migratory waterfowl. Roads and open fields in this area make it a good place for seeing wildlife. Plans are afoot to build observation towers here for visitors to watch the deer and bears.

Beginning about four miles south of the Alligator River Bridge on U.S. 64, the Gum Swamp area runs for 15 miles along the river's east bank. Motor vehicles and hunting dogs are forbidden here. Hunters must hike, boat or ride bicycles to reach this area.

A few miles south of Gum Swamp, the river bends to the west and offers another area for primitive hunting. Access is by water only.

East of U.S. Highway 264 hunting is allowed along 30 miles of the Croatan and Pamlico Sound shorelines, but the only dogs allowed are the retrievers of bird hunters. Numerous birds of prey are seen here, hawks, ospreys and eagles.

The southern flank of this refuge offers a different type of hunting experience. Jet fighters frequently roar by just above the treetops, en route to the ranges operated by the U.S. Air Force and Navy, where they practice their own hunting skills with rockets, bombs, cannons and machine guns.

Hunting is allowed on the perimeter road around the Navy range. The Air Force restricts hunters from their perimeter road because of secret laser tests, but hunting is allowed along roads leading into the facility. Signs abound warning of unexploded ordinance and blinding flashes from laser beams. If you have a cardiac pacemaker, keep clear of this area because of the extensive microwave radiation from the communications facilities.

All the bombing here apparently doesn't bother the deer, which are plentiful and large. It's almost as if the deer know that the target areas provide a sanctuary from hunters.

Jimmy Berry recalls hunting the ranges with his father. "Used to, they'd give you a permit on holidays to hunt the ranges. My daddy would go back there and turn the dogs loose. We'd drive right through the middle of the range by the targets. There'd be bombs laying in the road and we'd just drive around them. They were just smoke bombs anyway."

One area near the Alligator River refuge, Durant Island, at the mouth of the river, is privately owned and closed to the public.

For more information about the Albemarle-Pamlico area:

Alligator River National Wildlife Refuge
P.O. Box 1969
Manteo, N.C. 27954
(919) 473-1131
Call (800) 662-7137 to report wildlife violations.

Coastal Wildlife Refuge Society
P.O. Box 1808
Manteo, N.C. 27954
This is a group of volunteers dedicated to funding recreational and educational opportunities in the Alligator River and Pea Island refuges.

Goose Creek State Park
Route 2, Box 372
Washington, N.C. 27889
(919) 923-2191

Pettigrew State Park
Route 1, Box 336
Creswell, N.C. 27928
(919) 797-4475

Pocosin Lakes National Wildlife Refuge
Route 1, Box 195-B
Creswell, N.C. 27928
(919) 797-4431

Mattamuskeet/Swan Quarter National Wildlife Refuge
Route 1,Box N-2
Swan Quarter, N.C. 27885
(919) 926-4021

The Neuse and White Oak Rivers

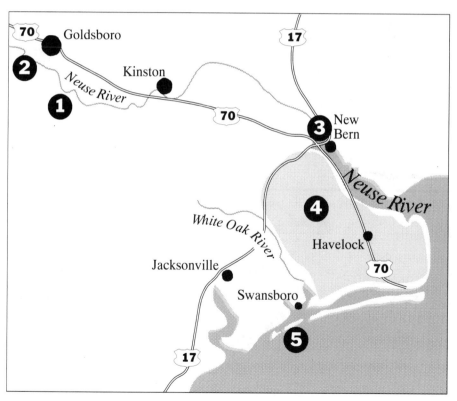

1. Cliffs of the Neuse State Park
2. Waynesborough State Park
3. Neuse River Game Lands
4. Croatan National Forest (area shown is approximate)
5. Hammocks Beach State Park

The Great Lake in Croatan National Forest.

L ocal hunters say stay out of Great Lake," said Ben Epting, a veteran sea kayaker from Bridgeton, "because the 'gators and snakes will eat you alive. I say, if you know what you're doing and use common sense, you can enjoy the special feeling of an unspoiled natural lake, completely surrounded by wilderness. Places like that are hard to find anymore."

Ben is a burly, bearded Outward Bound alumni who looks like a gentle Viking. He counsels troubled young people in New Bern by guiding them through the wilderness so they can gain confidence and self-esteem.

I took Ben's advice and paddled across that wild lake in the heart of the Croatan National Forest. I didn't see a single snake or 'gator, but I did see a lot of ospreys. The northeast wind blew hard and cold that April day. I guess the reptiles had better sense than to come out in that kind of weather, and I had the lake to myself.

The therapy of the wilderness is plentifully available in the area between the Neuse and White Oak Rivers.

Cliffs of the Neuse State Park

The geological history of the Neuse River is laid bare in the layers of a 90-foot-high cliff in a river bend at the edge of the coastal plain in Wayne County. It's all explained in the museum on top of the cliff.

The land around the cliff is an especially diverse habitat. Within a matter of minutes, hikers can walk through a cypress swamp forest dripping with moss and pass slopes covered with galax, a plant usually found in the mountains.

Tuscarora and Saponi warriors used this cliff as ceremonial ground and rendezvous point for hunting parties. Later settlers were drawn to the reported medicinal qualities of the water in seven springs in the vicinity. Visitors came to drink the healing waters, and the town of Whitehall grew into a lively resort at the springs before it burned in the 1920s. It was not rebuilt.

Local citizens proposed a park here in 1944, and the Cliffs of the Neuse State Park opened a year later. Gifts and purchases of land have expanded the park to its present 750 acres.

The park has an 11-acre lake and a campground with 35 sites for tents and trailers. Trails are short but all are different.

The park provides an interesting blend of three different types of forests, coastal swamp, longleaf pine and Piedmont hardwood. That concentrated diversity creates an unusual wildlife habitat. Bird lovers might get a glimpse of the northern parula that nests here in the abundant Spanish moss. Wood ducks live along the river and tributaries year-round. Hawks and bald eagles are often sighted. Occasional flights of mallards stop by in the winter.

Turtles and terrapins live in or near the water. Copperheads and cottonmouths are around, but most of the snakes seen here are non-venomous. Muskrats and otters can be observed swimming along the riverbank. Lizards scurry among the trees. Raccoons, opossums, rabbits, squirrels and deer inhabit the woods.

The museum does an exceptional job of interpreting the history of the park and its surroundings. Park rangers schedule guided hikes and other activities. Canoe trips down the Neuse are becoming popular, and the park offers good access to the river.

Waynesborough State Park

Upstream from Cliffs of the Neuse State Park is another, much smaller park, Waynesborough State Park near Goldsboro. It occupies only 142 acres and is open only during daylight hours. This land once was a thriving steamboat port and stagecoach junction before the railroad came through Goldsboro in 1839 and lured away the traffic. The town of Waynesborough, as the settlement was called, was torched by Yankee troops during the Civil War and never recovered. Goldsboro used the site as a landfill up until the 1970s. In 1979 the dump was covered and declared a state park.

It's used mostly as a picnic area. Restrooms, a gazebo and a pavilion are the only facilities. The park offers a pretty view of the river and a good spot to launch a canoe.

Neuse River Game Lands

This tiny hunting preserve in the river near New Bern is made up of six swampy islands covering only 120 acres. Owned and managed by the N.C. Wildlife Resources Commission, this area is used for duck hunting, fishing and wildlife observing. It can be reached only by boat from the landing at Glenburnie Park in New Bern.

Croatan National Forest

The Croatan National Forest sprawls over more than 158,000 acres southeast of New Bern between the Neuse and White Oak Rivers.

The alligator is just one of the many endangered species that thrive in the Croatan National Forest, which spreads over more than 158,000 acres between the Neuse and White Oak Rivers.

The longleaf pine, state tree of North Carolina, is plentiful in the Croatan National Forest.

Bounded by U.S. Highways 17 and 70 and N.C. Highways 58 and 24, this huge preserve is managed for recreation, timber and protection of endangered plants and wildlife.

Rare insect-eating plants such as the Venus flytrap and pitcher plant thrive here along with the red cockaded woodpecker, bald eagle and American alligator. Ospreys are doing so well here that biologists trap the birds for re-stocking in other areas.

Swamp forests, pine woods, tidal marshes and pocosin shrub bogs can be found within the Croatan Forest, along with five shallow lakes of mysterious origin. More than 150 miles of dirt and gravel roads allow easy access to some of this area.

The Neusiok Indians once occupied this wilderness, but they left behind little other than their name on the broad river that bounds the northeastern edge of the forest. The name of the forest itself was bestowed by President Franklin D. Roosevelt in 1936. Croatan is the Algonquin word for council town, the cryptic message found carved in a tree during the search for the fabled Lost Colony of Roanoke Island.

Neusiok and Tuscarora Indians lived here when the English first explored the river in 1585. John Lawson, the founder of Bath and surveyor general of the Carolina Colony, visited in 1705 and lived among the Tuscarora for a while. Then he set off on the famous "long march" into the interior of the Carolinas known only to Indians. He returned to England and published a book about his journey, *A New Voyage to Carolina*, a best seller in 1709 and still in print today. He returned to the river in 1710 with Baron von Graffenried to establish New Bern, a colony of Swiss emigrants on the site of the Indian town Chatooka.

The Indians were paid for the land but didn't understand the concept of buying and selling real estate. Tensions grew between the Indians and the settlers. In September of 1711, Lawson, accompanied by Von Graffenried, made his last canoe trip up the Neuse River. He didn't know the Indians were planning a major attack – designed to rid Carolina of the white menace once and for all. The unfortunate travelers were captured. Lawson was blamed for bringing more whites to abuse the Indians. He was executed in a grisly manner, his skin pierced with pine splinters that were then set on fire before his throat was cut with his own shaving razor. He became the first casualty of the Tuscarora War. Von Graffenried managed to talk his way to freedom with promises of better treatment for the Indians.

It was a bloody dawn in eastern Carolina on September 22, 1711. Indian war parties intent on genocide raided white settlements and killed every man, woman and child they could find. New Bern was spared at first, because of the deal Von Graffenried made with the Tuscarora, but that didn't last. Surviving whites gathered to build fortifications and organize militias for protection. South Carolina forces came to the rescue. The Indians weren't defeated until 1713 when South Carolina Indian mercenaries commanded by Colonel James Moore captured Neoheroka, the Tuscarora stronghold 30 miles upriver from New Bern.

Most of the Swiss settlers moved away from New Bern after the war, but the town recovered to become a major port. After the Revolutionary War, New Bern became the first capital of North Carolina.

When the Civil War began, New Bern was the second largest city on the coast. In 1862, Union General Ambrose Burnside was fresh from his victory at Roanoke Island, and New Bern was next on his list of conquests. He launched an amphibious assault at Slocum Creek on March 13, and marched on the city, encountering stiff resistance from outnumbered Confederates.

The Southern troops withdrew to New Bern and burned the Trent River bridge behind them. Union gunboats forced the Confederate troops to retreat by railroad to Kinston, and Union forces took the town on March 14, looting and pillaging as they went. New Bern stayed in federal hands until the end of the war, despite Confederate attempts to liberate the city in 1863 and 1864.

The Confederates built an ironclad ship, the Neuse, upriver near Kinston. But there wasn't enough water in the river to float it, so the ship remained at dock until it had to be partially destroyed to keep it from falling into Union hands. Part of the hull has been recovered and is now displayed at a state historic site near Kinston.

After the war, timbering, fishing and farming became the major sources of income for New Bern, until industries began to come to the eastern part of the state after World War II. The landscape changed as forests were cleared and swamps were drained. A pulpwood plant enriches New Bern's economy now but fouls the air. Downstream fish kills are common in the summer. But citizens have formed a group to take better care of the river.

Still, plenty of wilderness remains in the national forest and other preserves between the Neuse and White Oak Rivers, and anybody wanting to explore it should first visit the ranger station on U.S. Highway 70, where maps and information about trails, campsites and other facilities are available at no charge.

A swamp scene on Brice Creek in the Croatan National Forest.

Hunting is allowed in the Croatan Forest and is managed by the North Carolina Wildlife Resources Commission by agreement with the U.S. Forest Service.

"There's some nice deer in there," said Tommy Hughes. a state biologist who is in charge of eastern Carolina game lands. About 500 are harvested every year by licensed hunters with state permits.

Hunting for bears, small game and waterfowl also is good. A few areas are opening for turkey hunting, following successful stocking projects.

State workers plant about 200 acres as food plots for game and maintain waterfowl impoundments near Catfish Lake and along the White Oak River.

Fishing also is good in the forest waters. Instead of concentrating on the more glamorous largemouth bass, which can't tolerate the naturally acidic water of the Croatan lakes, fisheries biologist Barney Gyant wants to increase the catfish and yellow perch, which thrive in these waters.

He's doing extensive surveys of the waterways in the forest to find out what's there. Fish-attracting devices are submerged in the creeks and lakes and marked with buoys. These underwater structures – usually old logs – offer cover for fish and a food source for aquatic microorganisms, which attract small fish, which attract larger fish.

Boat access is provided at numerous spots within the forest, including Cahooque Creek on State Road 1717, where a big alligator lives near the landing. Other boat landings are at Brice Creek, on the northwestern edge of the forest, Haywoods Landing on the White Oak River and on Catfish Lake and Great Lake deep within the forest. Primitive camping is allowed without charge at all boat access areas.

At Brice Creek on State Road 1004 is a country store, Merchant's Grocery, where rugged aluminum canoes can be rented for just $10 a day fully equipped. They can be launched from the sandy cypress-lined beach behind the store.

To reach national forest land from the store, head upstream. A strong paddler can make it past the New Bern airport and to the forest boundary in about an hour. The water usually is calm but on warm weather weekends expect wakes from water skiers.

The shoreline progresses from marshgrass and shrubs to a magnificent bottomland forest shaded by cypress trees draped in Spanish moss. This is almost like a jungle river in places, with exotic flowers blooming along the tangled shore. Otters, muskrats, ospreys and great blue herons share the creek with snakes, turtles and alligators.

From Merchant's Store, it can take two to three hours of paddling – depending on your pace – to reach the Brice Creek Boating Access area, a good place for canoe camping. From here, it is possible to explore deeper into the swamps upstream. The Forest Service is planning to build a marked canoe trail along Brice Creek, possibly with floating platforms for camping deep in the swamp.

Several recreation areas along the Neuse River within the forest are easily reached from main roads. Fishers Landing is about eight miles south of New Bern on Forest Service Road 141 off U.S. 70. Turn at the Riverdale Mini-Mart. Camping is available at no charge. Picnic tables, toilets and drinking water are provided.

Neuse River Recreation Area, known locally as Flanner's Beach, is 11 miles south of New Bern off U.S. 70. The campground here has 22 sites nestled in a hardwood forest on a high bluff overlooking the Neuse with a vista of blue water and green shoreline. Drinking water, toilets, a dump station and invigorating cold showers are available at a charge of $7 per night. Wooden steps lead to the mile-long beach, where flounder gigging is popular on warm nights.

The best swimming beach within forest lands is off N.C. Highway

101 east of Havelock at Pinecliff Recreation Area. The beach is clean, the water blue and clear. Nearby is the state operated ferry at Cherry Branch offering free scenic crossings of the Neuse.

The Neusiok Hiking Trail begins at Pinecliff and stretches for 20 miles through the wilds to the Newport River. Primitive camping is permitted. Summertime hikers should be ready for bugs, heat and snakes. Parts of this trail can get overgrown but the Carteret County Wildlife Club has a maintenance program that tries to keep it clear.

Another recreation area is on the other side of the forest. Signs on N.C. Highway 58 north of Cape Carteret direct the way to the Cedar Point Recreation Area at the mouth of the White Oak River. The campground here has 50 wooded sites with toilets, picnic tables and drinking water beside the tidal marsh. A boat ramp provides access to the White Oak River, only eight miles from the ocean. Salt water fishing is especially good here.

The Cedar Point Tideland Trail is an easy one-mile walk through the marsh, with boardwalks in the boggy places. Fiddler crabs abound, quickly ducking into their holes at a walker's approach.

Wildlife viewing blinds are set along the trail, offering an excellent view of wading birds such as snowy egrets and great blue herons. In winter the blinds offer an opportunity to watch migratory waterfowl. Interpretive markers along the trail tell of the estuary's role as a nursery for sea life.

State Road 3065 on N.C. Highway 58 south of Maysville is a rough, sandy road that penetrates deep into the forest and dead ends at Great Lake, the largest of the five mysterious Croatan lakes. No one knows how these lakes were formed, perhaps from burning peat, perhaps from a meteor shower.

The road passes through longleaf pine forest and a designated pocosin wilderness area, where it is extremely easy to become disoriented. A bear hunter got lost in the pocosin near Catfish Lake in 1991, and it took more than 100 searchers and a helicopter three days to find him. There are four of these designated pocosin wilderness areas in the forest, covering more than 30,000 acres. Trails through these areas are few and may be overgrown. Only the most experienced and well equipped wilderness seekers should attempt these areas.

Great Lake is roughly four miles across. Like all the Croatan lakes, it's shallow with naturally acidic water. A swamp forest of gum and cypress grows on the eastern and southern shores.

The lake's facilities are basic: an unpaved boat ramp and parking area. A jeep path leads from the lake to a big field of wild blueberries and blackberries in an adjoining bear sanctuary. Bear tracks are common here, and the bears are often seen, especially in June when the berries usually ripen.

The Island Creek Forest Walk is a half-mile trail through a mature forest preserve, untouched by chainsaws, on State Road 1004 near Pollocksville. It was created in 1967 by the Trent Woods Garden Club of New Bern and the Forest Service. Interpretive brochures about the trail are available. James C. Simmons, Jr. of Scout Troop 67 in New Bern installed numbered posts to be used with the brochures as his Eagle Scout project.

This trail leads past full-grown yellow poplars, loblolly pines, bald cypress and several species of beech, gum, hickory and oak. Stream banks here are covered with stocking shaped Christmas Ferns. Partridge berry vines grow along the ground. Deer are often seen in the woods.

Hammocks Beach State Park

The 40-foot pontoon boat was loaded with fourth graders on a field trip as it pushed through the marsh. The boat followed a channel tramped out long ago by cattle that were herded across the marsh to the grasslands of Bear Island. An osprey flew past with a fish in its grip, causing the children to gasp and point in fascination.

More than 25,000 passengers take this 20-minute ferry ride each year, carrying from the civilization of the mainland landing at Hammocks Beach State Park near Swansboro to the wildness of Bear Island. This barrier island covers 892 acres and has dunes that tower 60 feet over maritime forest, shrub thickets and pristine beaches.

The only structures on the island are a classroom, bath house and barracks for park workers. That's all the development that ever will ever be on this island, which can be reached only by boat.

This island was once the private hunting preserve of a New York neurologist, Dr. William Sharpe. John Hurst looked after the island for the doctor back in the 1930s. But John Hurst was a black, and some local bigots didn't like him being in such a position of responsibility. Threats were made until the doctor offered a thousand-dollar reward to anyone reporting harassment of Hurst. That took care of the problem.

Dr. Sharpe wanted to leave the island to his friend John Hurst when he died, but he agreed instead to leave it to a black teachers association to use for recreation. It was later acquired by the state and operated as state park for blacks until the legal segregation was ended. Now the park is open to all. John Hurst's grandson, Jessie Hines, is a park ranger now, carrying on a family tradition of looking after the island.

"The remote location of this park makes it unique," said Sam Bland, the park superintendent. "It's a place that's not for everyone. It's too remote for some people. You have to deal with this park on its own terms."

Private boaters can come all year and tie up at the bulkhead near the ferry dock or just run up on the beach. Experienced open water paddlers in suitable canoes and kayaks will have no problem making the two-and-a-half mile trip. The free ferry operates only from June 1 to Labor Day. Lines can get long some days. Rangers only allow a certain number of people to be on the island at one time and may turn people away if this capacity has been reached. This is needed to protect the visitors as well as the fragile habitats. Only the number of people who can be quickly evacuated in case of a sudden storm or other emergency are allowed.

"Best time to come is in the winter," said Bland. "You can penetrate deep into the interior of the island without the insects being so bad. Really explore the maritime forest and the shrub thicket. January is an ideal time to camp here."

Primitive campsites are numbered and scattered across the island. Campers must pay a fee and get a permit at the park office. Sites one through seven are convenient to the 3.5-mile beach and the bath house. Sites eight through 10 are close by the beach and easily reached from a lagoon on the northeast end of the island. These are popular with canoe campers. Sites 11 and 12 are near the Bogue Inlet, and 13 and 14 overlook the inlet. The campsites at the far end of the island are best reached by boat.

Three group campsites are within 300 yards of the bathhouse and less than 50 yards from the beach. Visitors should know that it's about a half mile from the ferry landing to the beach. Bring only what you can comfortably carry and wear good shoes. The sand gets blisteringly hot in the summer. A refreshment stand serves cold drinks in the summer.

The beach here is worth any trouble it takes to get to it. Sea birds work the waves. Dolphins and even whales frequently swim by just offshore. Loggerhead sea turtles swim ashore to nest here each sum-

A ghost crab at Hammock Beach State Park

mer, and to protect them camping is not allowed during the full moons of June, July and August. Rangers request that people walking the beach at night not use flashlights. Turtles are spooked by any light and will not nest if frightened away.

If you should see a turtle crawling up the beach it's okay to quietly watch from a distance. Nesting female turtles may weigh 250 pounds and usually lay more than 100 eggs. The eggs that don't get eaten by raccoons will hatch after two months. The hatchlings start life running through a gantlet of hungry ghost crabs to the ocean. Once in the water young turtles still aren't safe. Those that survive all the predators and other dangers can live to be 80 years old and weigh 400 pounds, but many are caught and drowned in shrimp nets or strangled by a plastic bag someone has tossed away. Turtle sightings should be reported to rangers immediately so that protective measures can be taken. Some 40 nests were known to hatch on these beaches in 1992 from 80 attempted nestings.

Although the heavily developed Bogue Banks lies to the north and the world's largest Marine Base to the south, this island remains wild, a National Natural Landmark.

?e information about the Neuse and White .ver areas:

Distr.. Ranger, U.S. Forest Service
435 Thurman Road, New Bern, N.C. 28560
(919) 638-5628
This office is open business hours Monday through Friday. Call Forest Watch (800) 222-1155 to report fire, vandalism or crime.

Craven County Convention and Visitors Bureau
219 Pollock St., P.O. Box 1413
New Bern, N.C. 28560
(919) 637-9400
Located in New Bern's historic district, this office offers information about lodging, dining, marinas, campgrounds and scenic attractions. Ask about the historic walking tour, Tryon Palace, Civil War Museum and boat tours of the river. New Bern is an excellent base for exploring Croatan National Forest.

Merchant's Grocery on State Road 1004 at Brice Creek bridge
Open from 6:00 am to 10:00 pm seven days per week.
(919) 633-4875
Canoe rentals, refreshments and fishing supplies available. Call ahead for special arrangements or groups.

Cliffs of the Neuse State Park
Route 2, Box 50
Seven Springs, N.C. 28578
(919) 778-6234
Also serves Waynesborough State Park

Hammocks Beach State Park
Route 2, Box 295
Swansboro, N.C. 28584
(919) 326-4881
Ferry runs daily June 1 to Labor Day, plus weekends in May and September.

The Cape Fear River

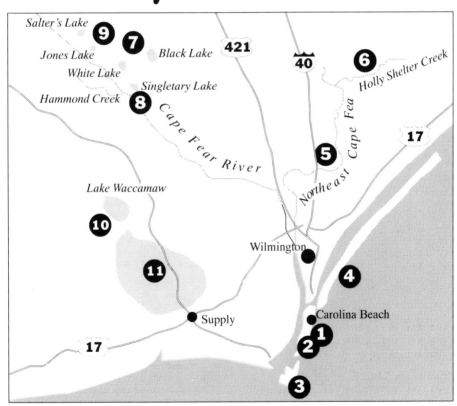

Salter's Lake
Jones Lake
White Lake
Black Lake
421
Hammond Creek
Singletary Lake
40
Holly Shelter Creek
Cape Fear River
Northeast Cape Fear
17
Lake Waccamaw
Wilmington
Supply
Carolina Beach
17

1. Carolina Beach State Park.
2. Fort Fisher State Recreation Area
3. Bald Head Island
4. Masonboro Island
5. Northeast Cape Fear River
6. Holly Shelter Swamp

7. Bladen Lakes State Forest
8. Singletary Lake State Park
9. Jones Lake State Park
10. Lake Waccamaw State Park
11. The Green Swamp (area shown
    is approximation)

A palm tree at Bald Head Island, the northern limit for this tree.

T he Cape Fear is a different river every day," said ferry captain Rodney Melton of Southport. "I never get tired of it." Melton has made the 20-minute run from Southport – hometown of the author Robert Ruark's grandfather – to Bald Head Island for 15 years and he considers it the best job he ever had. His vessel, the Revenge, was named for a wooden sailing ship once used by the buccaneer Stede Bonnet. This Revenge is a steel-hulled, diesel-powered passenger vessel, 65 feet long. It was built in Louisiana to haul workers to off-shore oil rigs. Now it carries wealthy passengers to their island vacation homes.

"Bald Head Island is one of the most beautiful places I've seen on Earth," said Melton. "It's unique. It's the cut-off point of the sub-tropical zone and has one of the last remaining maritime forests. Big variety of wildlife and plant life. The developer is trying to keep it in its pristine state and disturb it as little as possible."

Formerly called Smith Island, Bald Head got its name for a large bare sand dune visible from the sea. Sailors of old saw it only as a danger and a nuisance and called it the Cape of Fear. The island's cape resembles a shark fin jutting into the Atlantic. As it sinks beneath he waves, it becomes Frying Pan Shoals, a sandbar that stretches more than 20 miles offshore.

In his books about his outdoor adventures with his grandfather along the Cape Fear, *The Old Man and the Boy*, Robert Ruark tells of a fishing trip aboard a Coast Guard rum-chaser during Prohibition, where he and his grandfather encountered the dreaded shoals called Frying Pan.

These shoals were a perfect spot for pirates to trick ships into running aground during the early 1700s. The U.S. Coast Guard and modern navigation aids make the Cape Fear River much safer now. It's a 30-mile run upstream from the cape to Wilmington, the best deep-water port in the state and the largest city in eastern Carolina. Nearby beach towns such as Carolina, Kure and Wrightsville cater to the tourist trade and are crowded with condos, hotels, vacation homes and marinas.

Yet there are still places along the Cape Fear where Ruark and his grandfather would feel right at home riding around in a T-model Ford loaded with outdoor equipment and a jug of the Old Man's "nerve tonic."

The original residents of this river basin were a Siouan speaking tribe called the Cape Fear Indians by the white settlers. The natives lived off the land they called Chicora and minded their own business. A French expedition explored the area in 1524 and reported meeting the Indians.

The Spanish named the river Rio Jordan and planted a short-lived colony two years later. The Spaniards get credit for building the first known ship in North America during their brief stay.

Sir Richard Grenville reported that he almost lost his flagship to the shoals of Cape Fear while en route to settle Roanoke Island in 1586, but most historians believe he really was at Cape Lookout.

The English didn't attempt to live on the river until 1662, when William Hilton lead a group of Puritans from the Massachusetts Colony, but they didn't stay long and left a sign warning others to keep away. Englishmen from Barbados tried again in 1664 but the Indians ran them off after three years. It wasn't until 1715 that the badly treated Indians were conquered and almost wiped out.

Stede Bonnet was a former Royal Navy officer and planter from Barbados who – according to legend – got fed up with his nagging wife and turned to piracy. He roamed the coast and frequently used the Cape Fear as a hideout. He knew the waters well and exploited them to his advantage. His men set up lights on Frying Pan Shoals to fool captains into running aground so their vessels could be attacked and plundered. The pirates took 13 ships this way during the summer of 1718 alone. These were the glory years of piracy in the Carolinas for Bonnet and his good buddy Edward Teach, better known as Blackbeard.

English authorities sent Colonel William Rhett to clean up the Cape Fear in September of 1718. With two well armed sloops, the colonel caught the buccaneer at anchor and opened fire with 16 cannons. The pirate fought back but was outgunned and forced to surrender. Bonnet was taken to Charleston in chains, where he got a fair trial and a proper hanging.

With the sea lanes supposedly secure, the town of Brunswick was established in 1727 on the west bank of the Cape Fear. It was sacked by Spanish privateers in 1748. The colonial militia fought back and blew up a Spanish treasure ship, the Fortuna, then captured its cargo of gold and silver.

The town recovered and became home to Governor Arthur Dobbs in 1758, He caused a scandal by marrying a 15-year-old girl in 1762. Dobbs died three years later and was replaced by William Tryon.

It was a bad year for the new governor. Citizens were upset about the Stamp Act of 1765, a stiff English tax on all documents. Angry demonstrators surrounded his house to protest the injustice, a spark that ignited a revolutionary fire that smoldered for 10 years before it flared into war.

Governor Josiah Martin was forced to flee New Bern in 1775 and take refuge at Fort Johnston at the mouth of the Cape Fear. Cornelius Harnett led an attack on the fort but the governor escaped aboard an English ship. Martin plotted to retake the colony with a two-pronged attack. Scottish highlanders loyal to the crown were to march downriver from their settlement of Cross Creek (now Fayetteville) and link up with British troops coming by sea. Together they would take Wilmington, the port established in 1739 that had become the center of commerce on the Cape Fear.

The Highlanders were brave warriors and eager for a glorious battle. They got it when they were ambushed at the Moore's Creek bridge 25 miles north of Wilmington, where Robert Howe and James Moore lay in wait with two regiments of militia. Planks had been removed from the bridge and the remaining support timbers had been greased. The Highlanders charged across the slippery logs, yelling their battle cry, "King George and Broadswords," while drummers and bagpipers played. The well concealed Americans slaughtered them with small arms fire.

Wilmington was saved until January of 1781, when the British returned and occupied the town to maintain a base for Lord Cornwallis, the commander of all British forces. Cornwallis rested here after the Battle of Guilford Courthouse, then marched his troops to Virginia where they met defeat at the hands of General George Washington and the Continental Army at Yorktown. Cornwallis surrendered and the British forces withdrew. The colony was now a nation.

After the war, Wilmington continued to grow and prosper as a port supporting the plantation economy. Rice was a major crop grown in paddies beside the river. Fishing was – and still is – a big part of the Wilmington economy. Alligators were hunted for their valuable skins. Timber, naval stores and other forest products were shipped downriver from the interior of the state. Ocean-going vessels called here and steamboats hauled their cargo upriver to Fayetteville. The railroad came through in 1840 and linked the port to Virginia and the northeastern states. The town of Brunswick was abandoned by 1830 and the ruins are now a state historic site.

When the Civil War started, Wilmington was a strategic prize, heavily defended by the Confederates. Several forts were built around the river, with Fort Fisher – called the Gibraltar of the South – being the strongest.

Twenty-four cannons were mounted on earthworks 25 feet thick at Fort Fisher, providing covering fire for blockade runners to get past the Union warships that patrolled offshore.

Blockade runners were free-lance smugglers in fast steamships that carried cotton overseas to trade for weapons and supplies. By 1864, Wilmington was the only Southern port still open and the only Confederate link to the rest of the world.

Union forces delivered a holiday greeting on the night before Christmas Eve in 1864. A worn out steamer was packed with explosives, then beached at the fort and detonated. But the explosion failed to breach the earthworks. Gunboats shelled the fort with little effect. Ground forces commanded by General Benjamin Butler attacked on Christmas and got within 50 yards of the fort, but retreated in such a hurry that men were left behind. Confederate General William Lamb and his troops celebrated their Christmas victory.

Butler was replaced by the bolder General Alfred Terry and the Union attacked again on January 13, 1965. The river was full of Yankee gunboats that shelled the fort continuously for three days and nights. Ground forces attacked on January 15, and penetrated the Southern defenses. Outnumbered and outgunned, the Confederates fought with anything they could get their hands on. General Lamb was wounded in the hellish fight and his second in command was forced to surrender. Meanwhile, Confederate General Braxton Bragg sat near Wilmington with 6,000 troops and failed to reinforce his comrades. Federal troops took Wilmington on February 22, cutting off the last supply line to Richmond and the last hope of the Confederacy. The war ended two months later.

After the war, Wilmington didn't grow much until the 1960s when manufacturing and tourism began adding to the traditional industries of logging, farming and fishing. Chemical plants now line the river upstream from Wilmington. A nuclear power plant with the worst safety record in the country operates sometimes at Southport. All this development polluted once pristine waters and leveled forests. Swamps were drained an cleared. The completion of Interstate Highway 40 no doubt will bring more visitors and residents to the lower Cape Fear, further draining its resources.

For now, however, enough wild territory remains in the river's basin to give today's equivalent of the Old Man and the Boy places where they still can roam.

Carolina Beach State Park

Carolina Beach State Park was established in 1969 with land purchased by the state and donated by the U.S. Army Corps of Engineers. It's a natural oasis in the heavily developed peninsula between the ocean the river.

This 1,773-acre preserve hosts more than 150,000 visitors each year. Leo Dillard, a Raleigh native and veteran ranger, has managed the park for 13 years. His jurisdiction also includes the Fort Fisher State Recreation Area and 1,200 acres of marsh on Bald Head Island.

"I like it down east," he said. "Hunting, fishing, always something going on outdoors."

He likes fall best at the park, because it is less crowded than in spring and summer, yet the weather remains warm and the fishing is good.

Fishing is a major activity here, and the park boasts a brand new marina complete with bait and tackle shop. There are 65 slips for docking boats and two ramps offering access to the river. From here boaters can head upriver, along the Intracoastal Waterway or out to sea. Rough water is common here, though, and there's a large sandbar just offshore from the marina. "We have a lot of boats getting hung up on that thing," said Leo Dillard.

Alligators occasionally swim through the marina's basin but they don't bother anyone.

Bank fishers here take trout, flounder, croaker and an occasional puppy drum by bottomfishing with shrimp or cut bait. Some anglers like to fish the deep waters of Snow's Cut from the high bank about 300 yards behind the camping area. It can be hazardous. Several people fishing here have drowned after falling off the bank.

The campground has 83 drive-in sites in a shady oak and pine forest. All are equipped with picnic tables and grills. Water points are located throughout, and two pump stations are provided for RVs. Two centrally located bathhouses have hot water showers and are heated in cold weather.

Scouts and other youth groups can use the two group camping areas alongside the Swamp Trail. Hand-pumped water, tables, latrines and fireplaces are provided.

Raccoons are getting to be a nuisance around the campsites. Campers are warned to keep food in closed containers and to be wary of the raccoons, which can carry rabies.

The park has five miles of well marked hiking trails, and maps and

The Sugarloaf Trail, above, runs through Carolina Beach State Park, through marshes and forests to the top of a 60-foot sand dune. Also in the park is Flytrap Trail, where Venus flytraps, right, and other rare plants are found in abundance.

information about current trail conditions are available at the ranger station.

The Sugarloaf Trail runs from the marina parking lot alongside the river through marshes and pine forest to the top of a 60-foot dune. Windswept live oak trees grow atop this mound of white sand called Sugarloaf. The dune dominates the landscape and has always been a major navigational landmark on the river. Confederate forces used it for a lookout and watched the fall of Fort Fisher from this sandy perch. It's an ideal place to get away. Binoculars are helpful here. The view is magnificent and pelicans fly past at eye level.

The trail continues from the dune past three natural ponds, all different. The first is Cypress Pond, an exquisite miniature swamp forest of young cypress. Next is Lily Pond with its surface almost completely covered with water lilies. The final pond is called the Grass Pond and, yes, it's full of grass. Quietness and patience might be rewarded with a glimpse of an alligator or otter in one of the ponds.

Between the park office and campground just off the main road is the Flytrap Trail, an easy half-mile loop. Venus flytraps and other rare plants are found here in abundance. This park has the greatest concentration of these bug-eating plants for 50 miles around. These delicate flowers are small, close to the ground and easily damaged so walk with caution. It is illegal to molest them.

The Snow's Cut Trail follows the waterway between the picnic area and the campground. Brown pelicans are numerous here year-round. Winter brings waterfowl. Ospreys fish in Snow's Cut during the summer. A wide variety of songbirds migrate through the park in spring and fall.

Other wildlife apt to be seen along the trails include, lizards, skinks, snakes, squirrels and marsh rabbits, maybe even a deer.

This park offers quite a contrast to the city at its back and the garish beach towns on its flanks, and plans are in the works to expand it.

Fort Fisher State Recreation Area

Five miles south of Carolina Beach State Park is the Fort Fisher State Recreation Area. Close by are the state aquarium, the Fort Fisher historic site and the state ferry to Southport. Here are four miles of public beach, some of it lined with live oak trees. Waves break here over coquina outcrops, the only naturally rocky area on the North Carolina coast.

The story of the Battle of Fort Fisher and the blockade runners is

At Fort Fisher Recreation Area, waves break over coquina outcrops, the only naturally rocky area on the North Carolina coast.

The Fort Fisher aquarium staff lead a canoe trip to Zeke's Island Estuarine Preserve.

told at the nearby museum. The earthworks of the fort remain and visitors can climb them, but they are threatened as the ocean continues to erode the old fort. It's unlikely that Fort Fisher will survive this final battle with the sea, but supporters want the state to change the coastal protection laws and build a jetty to try to stop the erosion.

The Fort Fisher aquarium not only displays marine life of the Carolina coast but offers a full schedule of field trips. Aquarium staff members, usually marine biologists or naturalists, lead canoe trips to Zeke's Island Estuarine Preserve nearby.

"Every trip is different," said Gail Miller, education coordinator for the aquarium. "We try to promote awareness of the estuarine environment. We do some birdwatching, maybe some crabbing or surf fishing. It's a very casual trip, suitable for parents and children."

The aquarium offers other activities including surf fishing lessons, crabbing, clamming, salt marsh exploration, and arts and crafts programs. Call in advance to arrange canoe trips for groups of 10 or more.

Gail Miller and her co-workers are expanding their family-oriented field trips. In the works are canoe trips on the Black River – a tributary of the Cape Fear and home to a 1,600-year-old Cypress forest, the oldest trees east of the Mississippi. These swamp giants can be viewed from the river just upstream from the bridge on N.C. Highway 53 about 25 miles north of Wilmington.

Bald Head Island

On my first trip to Bald Head Island, I paddled through the salt marsh to the back side of the island, setting my course by the weathered lighthouse called Old Baldy. When the water got shallow I just waded with boat in tow. Terns flew over the islands in the marsh. Pied oyster catchers worked the shellfish mounds and scrambled when I got close. On my way back through the marsh, I took a wrong turn and ended up in the roisterous Cape Fear River at the mouth of the ocean.

I stuck it out and paddled through rough water to the rock jetty that connects the mainland to Zeke's Island, near the northern edge of Bald Head Island. After a hard landing, I hauled the boat over the rocks and into the shallow, protected water of the basin. Not the safest way to go. Only dedicated open water paddlers should try it.

The easiest way to get to Bald Head is on the private ferries that run from the Indigo Plantation landing across the river near Southport. Once there, the only transportation is by foot, electric golf cart or bicycle (cart, bikes and canoes can be rented at the marina) but trams

Timber Creek runs through the middle of Bald Head Island, a semi-tropical island, the only such island in the entire state.

pulled by gas-powered micro vans carry visitors and their luggage back and forth from the dock.

A maritime forest covers 800 of the island's 13,000 acres, and much of it is now developed with houses, condominiums (more than 400 different units) and a golf course complete with alligators in the lagoons. For more information about the island, see the listing at the end of this chapter. About 70 people now live on the island, but seasonal visitors increase that number significantly.

The beaches on Bald Head are not developed, and they provide the most productive loggerhead turtle nesting area in the state, thanks to the work of the Bald Head Conservancy. A biologist and naturalists work from the old lighthouse keeper's house to see that the hatchling turtles have every chance to survive.

A short nature trail gives a brief sample of the semitropical heart of the island, where palm trees and live oaks rustle in the wind. Timber Creek runs through the middle of the needlerush marsh that rings with the calls of clapper rails.

The state-owned part of the island is mostly marsh, but 200 acres of the rare semi-tropical forest have been set aside by the conservancy as a preserve.

Bald Head once was home only to lighthouse keepers and the occupants of a U.S. Lifesaving station. A Confederate fort stood here during the Civil War. Later owners of the island wanted to build a bridge, but the state refused to issue permits. Environmentalists sued in the 1970s to prevent the marina from being built but lost. There was talk about making the island a state park years ago, but the money for it never came through. Bald Head would have been a magnificent state park, a crown jewel for the state, but the state's citizens have to be content now with a few hundred acres of marsh on this once-wild semitropical island, the only such island in the entire state.

Masonboro Island

Squeezed between the garish tourist strips of Wrightsville Beach and Carolina Beach is an undeveloped island called Masonboro, a narrow strip of sand, dune grasses and marsh that stretches for 8.4 miles.

This island, no more than 1,000 feet wide and far narrower at many points, is owned by the state as an estuarine preserve.

The beach here is beautiful and great for surf fishing. The marshes behind the island harbor a wide diversity of bird and marine life. Smaller nearby islands created by the ongoing dredging of the Intracoastal Waterway behind Masonboro are sprouting stands of maritime forest and attracting nesting shorebirds and other wildlife, such as raccoons and deer. Ospreys can be seen in the marsh, as well as endangered peregrine falcons, and loggerhead turtles nest on the beaches.

No bridge connects this island to the mainland but hordes of pleasure boaters descend in summer – especially during the Fourth of July weekend. Fall is the best time to visit. The insects and crowds are gone then and fishing is at its best. Boaters heading for Masonboro should be alert for shallow water and sand bars.

Northeast Cape Fear River and Holly Shelter Swamp

The Northeast Cape Fear River intersects the Cape Fear at Wilmington, but only a few miles upstream this classic black water river passes through a genuine wilderness lined with cypress, populated by very large alligators, the Holly Shelter Swamp.

Hunting and fishing are done for fun along the river and through the swamp now, but some people remember when these activities were vital here.

More than 48,000 acres of swamps and woodlands along the Northeast Cape Fear River have been set aside as the Holly Shelter Game Lands, where barred owls, right, can be found. The river itself is excellent for paddling, below.

The late Hallie Dale used to live in Wilmington, but he grew up near this river during the Depression.

"It was a lot different in the woods back then, had all those big old trees with hardly any underbrush. We'd hunt deer, coons, squirrels, rabbits and ate everything we killed.

"Good fishing here if you knew how. We used cane poles and those black earthworms we dug out of the swamp. Used to jigger fish with artificial lures too. Take a limber cane pole, put about 18 inches of line on the end and tie on a double bladed spinner with a guinea feather. We'd work that lure under the river banks and catch what we called green trout. They call them largemouth bass today.

"I reckon those were the best years of my life. I guess we were poor, but we didn't know it because everyone else was just as poor as we were."

The river itself is little different now than it was when Hallie Dale was growing up, but the swamp and the woods have changed greatly. Most of the big trees have been logged out and a wildfire burned through the area in 1987. The forest is recovering nicely but it is tangled with brush and small trees, making movement difficult for hunters but providing good cover for game.

More than 48,000 acres of swamps and woodlands along the river have been set aside as the Holly Shelter Game Lands. Deer are abundant here, especially in the ridges between the pocosins, and the area is crowded with hunters in deer season. Small game hunting and bear hunting also are excellent. The Wildlife Resources Commission plants more than 100 acres as food for game. Duck hunting is good along Ashes Creek and nearby impoundments, but Ashes Creek can be risky for dogs, because numerous alligators more than 10 feet in length live there.

A boating access ramp is near the wildlife depot on State Road 1520 for those who want to fish or canoe along the river or the many creeks that lead back into the swamps. Wood ducks and owls are frequently seen in the swamps.

Hikers are welcome in the game land but should avoid the area during hunting season. The dirt roads through the preserve are the best places for hiking. Lodge Road starts at the gate near the depot and runs 25 miles. It comes out on Highway17 about four miles north of Hampstead. An easy trail follows the river levee.

Venus flytraps and pitcher plants can be seen here. Remember that it is against the law to possess them. The fine can be as much as $500 per plant for the first offense, $1,000 per plant for a second offense, and civil penalties also are possible. Birders can see red cockaded woodpeckers on the east side of the preserve where the longleaf wiregrass grows. Known nesting trees are marked with white bands. Look for them along the ridges. Permits can be obtained for camping and other special activities.

Horses are not allowed here, but in 1991, nearly 100 horseback riders showed up on the last day of muzzleloading season, disrupting the hunt and causing an angry confrontation with hunters.

A turpentine still is on display at Bladen Lakes State Forest, where an exhibit shows how tar, pitch and turpentine were made.

Bladen Lakes State Forest

At one time, more than 11 million acres of longleaf pines grew in North Carolina. Fewer than 400,000 acres remain. All the rest were cut for timber and production of naval stores such as tar, pitch and turpentine.

One longleaf pine forest on the Cape Fear River was logged out in the 19th century, then used to raise cotton until the soil was depleted in the 1930s. This land fell into the hands of the state during the Depression, and to provide jobs, the state decided to let the Civilian Conservation Corps turn it into a state forest.

Now some of this land is being used to restore the longleaf pine in North Carolina. The first seed orchard for these trees was established here in 1966 and seedlings have been replanted across the state.

Bladen Lakes State Forest now covers 32,237 acres along the river in Bladen County near Elizabethtown. Tree farming is the main activity within the forest, and most of this land is covered with pines. But several shallow lakes known as Carolina Bays are within the forest and these areas, as well as stands of turkey oaks, have been left natural.

Part of the forest is managed as a game preserve and hunting for deer, bears, birds and small game is allowed. A wild turkey restoration project is under way in the forest but hunting is not yet allowed for turkeys. Primitive camping is allowed in the game lands except for state parks and educational forests.

More than 140 miles of sandy roads offer access to the forest. Most are well maintained, but four-wheel-drive vehicles may be needed for some side roads, particularly in bad weather. Gates are open only during business hours on weekdays.

Eight hundred acres of this forest near the intersection of State Road 1511 and Highway 242 and four miles north of Elizabethtown are reserved for education and research. Exhibits here show, among other things, how tar, pitch and turpentine were made. A huge turpentine still is on display. Markers along the Turnbull Creek Trail here explain forestry. Special programs for classes and groups can be scheduled in advance.

Singletary Lake State Park

Two state parks are within the boundaries of Bladen Lakes State Forest, both built by Civilian Conservation Corps workers in the '30s.

Singletary Lake State Park is in the southeastern corner of the forest, just off N.C. Highway 53. This park is primarily for group campers and is frequently used by Scout groups, 4-H clubs and other such groups. It is closed to individuals when groups are using the rustic camp facilities, but individuals may use the park during daylight hours when no groups are present.

Singletary Lake covers 572 acres and parts of it are lined by 400-year-old cypress trees. A wooden pier stretches 500 feet into the water.

Two camps are within the park. Camp Ipecac, built in 1939 and named for the poison antidote plant found in the park, has 10 cabins, a mess hall and bathhouse by the lake with a big sand beach. It can accommodate up to 88 in warm weather, but it is closed in winter because the buildings are not heated.

Camp Loblolly Bay is a smaller but more modern, built in 1984. It's heated, open year-round and is wheelchair-accessible.

Fees are charged for both camps, and reservations are required.

Activities at the park include swimming (no lifeguards), canoeing and hiking. Rangers provide guided hikes and nature study programs for campers on request.

Jones Lake State Park

Jones Lake State Park, the second park within Bladen Lakes State Forest, was built as a segregated facility for black people, but now, of course, is open to all. It is in the northwest corner of the forest, off N.C. Highway 242.

The heart of this park is a lake with 2.2 miles of shoreline, a white sand beach and shady stands of cypress. Trees growing at an odd angle near the picnic area were blown over by Hurricane Hazel in 1954. Many family reunions and other social gatherings are held regularly on the big picnic grounds. Canoeing and sailing are popular on the lake, and small rowboats may be rented at the pier.

The beach is crowded on summer weekends and holidays, but those who want to escape the crowds can do so at this park. A much smaller and isolated Carolina Bay, Salters Lake, is also in this park. A locked gate prevents access to this 120-acre lake, but directions to it and keys to the gate are available at the ranger's office.

A canoe is perfect for this lake. Flights of wood ducks often can be seen here, and the lakeshore is home to the endangered pine barrens treefrog. Fishing is not particularly good because of the acidic water, but catfish and yellow perch can be caught. Cottonmouths also abide here, so caution is advised.

A three-mile trail follows the shoreline around Jones Lake and offers a good look at the diverse Carolina Bay habitat. Migratory ducks can be seen on the lake and vultures roost at the lake's northern edge. Red cockaded woodpeckers, hawks and barred owls also live along the lake. Deer, bears and bobcats are sometimes seen or heard in the dense woods. A one-mile loop nature trail with interpretive markers provides an interesting walk near the campground. The campground has 20 sites with a central bathhouse with hot showers. It is open from mid-March until mid-November and a fee is charged.

Rangers conduct guided hikes and other activities at the park.

Lake Waccamaw State Park

Lake Waccamaw is by far the biggest of the Carolina Bays, covering nearly 9,000 acres in Columbus County, just off U.S. Highway 74-76, about 20 miles southwest of the Cape Fear River. The Waccamaw-Siouan Indians who live near this lake are known as the People of the Falling Star, and they believed that this lake was created by a falling star, perhaps a great meteorite.

A state park was established on 1,508 acres on the southeastern

Father and son fish on Lake Waccamaw, where a multitude of fresh water fish thrive.

shore of the lake in 1976, and the park also includes the entire lake. This is a little-used park with bare facilities. Picnic tables sit under live oaks dripping with moss. Hike-in campsites have tables and a pretty view of the lake but campers have to bring everything else – including drinking water. A boardwalk leads to a pier with a panoramic view of the water. A trail network follows old logging roads covered in deer tracks.

Boating of all types is popular on this lake. There is a public boat ramp two miles north of the park entrance on Bella Coola Road. There is additional access by commercial marinas on Lake Shore Drive. You can launch a canoe at the mouth of Waccamaw River near the dam.

Fishing is also popular. The lake's water isn't as acidic as that in most other Carolina Bays. A multitude of fresh water fish thrive here, including some species of minnows found nowhere else. Fishing is good. White perch school early in the morning in late spring, and when the schools are found many fish can be caught quickly. Largemouth bass prowl the grass beds. Alligators occasionally venture into the lake, but they usually keep to the swamps and creeks around the lake's edge.

Perhaps the best place to see alligators here is from a car. Many live in the canals along the road leading to the park, State Road 1947

(Lake Shore Drive). Big ones are seen frequently in warm months. An alligator once snatched a German shepherd running along this road with his owner. Wildlife officers attempted to capture the alligator and relocate it but it put up such a fight that they were forced to kill it.

The Green Swamp

Lake Waccamaw provides the headwaters for the Waccamaw River, a narrow, black-water stream that twists and turns 120 swampy miles to Winyah Bay near Georgetown, South Carolina.

A canoe is the only way to explore the first 10 miles of the river as it passes through the Green Swamp. The channel sometimes disappears as the river threads its way through thick swamp forest. Getting lost is easy. The scenery, though, makes this trip worthwhile.

Flocks of the rare, curve-billed white ibis are sometimes spotted here. Wood ducks live in the swamp year-round. This is said to be the snakiest place on earth, and alligators are common.

About five map miles downstream from the lake in the center of the swamp is the isolated community of Crusoe Island. People here are thought to be descendants of shipwrecked Portuguese sailors, although some think they may be descendants of the Lost Colonists of Roanoke Island. No one really knows where they came from, but like Carolina Cajuns, they've made a nice home for themselves in the swamp.

Etthemer Spivey and his son Tommy run a hunting and fishing guide service on Crusoe Island and still live off the land by farming, trapping and catching snakes.

"This river has fed many a hungry belly," Etthemer Spivey said.

Spivey loved the river and the swamp so much that in the 1960s he went to battle against timber companies that were spraying chemicals over the swamp. He was convinced that the sprays were polluting the water, killing fish and other wildlife. When he confronted timber company officials he was met with a shrug.

"They told me they were in the timber business, not the fish raising business. I said, 'We'll just see about that.'"

Spivey's hunting clients included some well-connected politicians. He called on his buddies in Raleigh and the timber companies soon ceased their spraying.

The companies' primary activity never was restricted, however, and the giant cypress stumps throughout the swamp are sad testament to that. Most of the swamps old-growth trees have been cut and much of the swamp has been ditched and converted to farm land. But big

Ossie Jacobs, a retired Baptist
minister, has lived in the Green
Swamp for more than 80 years.
Jacobs, a descendent of the
Woccon Indians, lives beside an
old Indian trail, now a dirt road,
that leads to the shore of Lake
Waccamaw.

chunks of the swamp remain, however, despite generations of exploita-
tion, and all through it cypress saplings have sprouted. And Tommy
Spivey intends to continue living in the swamp, prowling in a dugout
canoe, hunting and fishing just as his father and grandfather did before
him.

He is not alone in his hope for the swamp's future.

Ossie Jacobs, a retired Baptist minister, has lived in the swamp for
more than 80 years, just as his ancestors did for more than 200 years
before him. Jacobs is descended from the Woccon Indians who fled to
the swamp early in the 18th Century after warring with white settlers in
what is now South Carolina. He lives beside an old Indian trail – now a
dirt road – that leads to the shore of Lake Waccamaw, where his ancestors once had their council ground. Many of his ancestors were hunted
down and massacred during the Cape Fear Indian Wars of 1715, their
bodies piled into mass graves near the lake. But some managed to survive in the swamp, and eventually they adopted the language and ways
of the settlers.

"They had everything it took to enjoy life," Jacobs says of the
ancestors he honors. "They were not savage, they were not ignorant.

They knew there was a creator over them. Now we have the Christian religion and all of these modern inventions, and a lot of it is good, but some of it is hurtful. Some of it is destroying the nature that God intended man to have."

Jacobs tells of hearing wolves howling and panthers screaming when he was growing up in the swamp, creatures long since killed off. He recalls fishing trips when his people waded the shallow water of Lake Waccamaw, muddying it up with sticks so fish would surface to escape the turbid water and could be quickly grabbed by hungry hands. As a young man he and his friends would journey up the river and camp in wigwams built of saplings and straw while they hunted for deer and other game. He remembers traditional funerals in the swamp.

"My people didn't bury their dead," he says. "We placed them on scaffolds in a sacred part of the forest so the Great Spirit could get them and take them to the happy hunting grounds."

He still can hear the forlorn chanting and pounding of drums that echoed through the swamp during those ceremonies.

Much has changed in the swamp since Jacobs' boyhood, but his people, he thinks, will always be here, and so, he hopes, will the swamp.

Some steps have been taken to ensure that the hopes of Jacobs and others will be fulfilled. About 15,000 acres of the Green Swamp along N.C. Highway 211 near Supply are now owned by the North Carolina Nature Conservancy. The protected area includes swamp, a longleaf pine forest and savanna grasslands. A number of unusual plants are found here, including sundew, pitcher plants, venus flytraps and some rare orchids and lilies. A few stands of Atlantic white cedar also grow here. Littering and poaching of rare plants trouble this preserve, and if it continues public access may be shut off. Conservancy volunteers conduct guided field trips here several times a year. Hunters with gamelands permits may hunt here in season.

The Green Swamp has long inspired stories of ghosts, voodoo and root doctors casting spells, but it casts its own spell on visitors.

The spirits of Robert Ruark and his grandfather, the Old Man and the Boy, still haunt this swamp and all the remaining wilderness of the Cape Fear basin.

For more information about the Cape Fear area:

Carolina Beach State Park
PO Box 475
Carolina Beach, N.C. 28428
(919) 458-8206 (office)
(919) 458-8207 (marina)
This office also manages state owned land at Fort Fisher and Bald Head Island. Special programs and tours held through the year for groups with advance notice.

N.C. Aquarium/Fort Fisher
PO Box 130
Kure Beach, N.C. 28449
(919) 458-8257
Marine life exhibits and field trips on foot and by canoe. Call for current schedule. Hike to the beach on the Hermit Trail.

Fort Fisher Historic Site
PO Box 68
Kure Beach, N.C. 28449
(919) 458-5538
Museum displays Civil War artifacts and offers audio-visual program. Stroll to the top of the earthworks to enjoy the view, dine in the shady picnic area or enjoy the beach.

Bald Head Island
(800) 234-1666
Information about ferries, real estate sales and rentals. There are about 30 condominium units available for rent. Rent ranges from $800 to $1200 per week, depending on the season, summer rates being higher. Store, clubhouse, bar. Bicycle, golf cart and canoe rentals available on the island. Ferry leaves Indigo Plantation every hour near Southport. Round-trip rates, including luggage, are $15 for adults and $8 for children 12 and under. $10 fee for bicycle, surfboard or other bulky cargo. Call for current schedule.

Bald Head Island Conservancy
Bald Head Island, N.C. 28461
(919) 457-7350
Membership information. Schedule of turtle walks, alligator walks, birding and fishing events.

Bladen Lakes Educational State Forest
Route 2, Box 942-A
Elizabethtown, N.C. 28337
(919) 588-4161
800 acre enclave within 32,237 acre State Forest. Self guided trails and forestry exhibits. Special programs on request. Office will provide hunting information for the rest of the state forest that is managed as gamelands. Basically, sportsmen with gamelands permits can hunt the entire Bladen Lakes State Forest except for marked safety zones around the Educational State Forest, Jones Lake and Singletary Lake state parks. This is the place to begin your exploration of the largest state forest in North Carolina.

Jones Lake State Park
Route 2,Box 945
Elizabethtown, N.C. 28337
(919) 588-4550
Hiking, camping, swimming, boating, picnic areas and two Carolina Bay lakes next to Bladen Lakes State Forest.

Singletary Lake State Park
Route 1, Box 63
Kelly, N.C. 28488
(919) 669-2928
Group cabin camps available by reservation next to Bladen Lakes State Forest. This office also manages the Lake Waccamaw State Park.

Cape Fear Coast Convention and Visitors Bureau
PO Box 1810
Wilmington, N.C. 28403
(919) 341-7815 or (800) 222-4757
Tourist attractions, accommodations and special events in the lower Cape Fear area. Ask about paddlewheel riverboat rides on the Henrietta II from the Wilmington waterfront.

North Carolina Nature Conservancy
PO Box 805
Chapel Hill, N.C. 27514
(919) 967-7007
Owners of Green swamp preserve. Ask for schedule of guided field trips. Managed for hunting as a gameland in cooperation with N.C.

Wildlife Resources Commission. Call (919) 638-3000 for game lands information.

Waccamaw-Siouan Development Association
PO Box 221
Bolton, N.C. 28423
(919) 655-8778
Tribal office. Native crafts for sale at near-by trading post. Fall Pow-wow attracts Indian dancers from all over North America. The celebration is open to the public and offers traditional foods, crafts and art. It's a colorful history lesson and a terrific family outing. Don't miss it! Call for directions and schedule.

Acknowledgements

A lot of good people really helped me with this book and I'd like to offer my sincere thanks.

My wife, Gwen, held down the home front while her old man was off wandering the wilds, and joined me whenever she could. We've traveled some long, wild trails together – and we'll do more!

My 12-year-old son, Eric, served as assistant photo editor and trail boss. He helped me find owls, alligators and Venus flytraps. He'll be a fine man one day, if I can keep him from running off and living in the wilderness like Tarzan!

My best friend R.C. always left the door open for me at his Tar River retreat and offered support in ways too numerous to list.

Whiting Toler was my high school art teacher. He still has time to listen to my ideas and offer his support.

Bill Black, editor of the Outdoor Scene, gave me the assignment that started it all.

Fred Bonner, the editor of Carolina Adventure, took me fishing and hunting, told me I was a journalist, then put me to work and made me prove it.

A special thanks to all of the conservation professionals: rangers, biologists, technicians, managers, information officer and so many others who always found time to answer my many questions cheerfully. A big thanks to all of those hundreds of people that I men and talked with around the trails, waterways, campgrounds, marinas and hunting lodges of my native land. They all had something to share.

I offer my thanks and awe to Jerry, Beth and Elizabeth, the craftsmen of Down Home Press. They worked wonders with my raw material.

Finally, to you, the reader. Thanks for picking up this book. I hope you enjoy it and find some happiness between these pages. Maybe we'll meet on the trail some day and share stories.

C

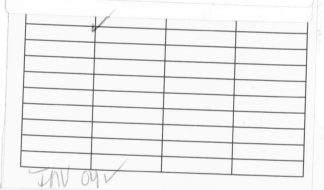

INV 04

INV 14